KINGDOMS AND CONQUESTS

The Ancient Near East 931-586 B.C.

Shawn E. Kauffeld

NORTHWESTERN PUBLISHING HOUSE
Milwaukee, Wisconsin

The cover and interior illustrations were originally executed by James Tissot (1836-1902). The map on page 127 is the work of NPH artist Duane Weaver.

Library of Congress Card 89-63677
Northwestern Publishing House
1250 N. 113th St., P.O. Box 26975, Milwaukee, WI 53226-0975
© 1990 by Northwestern Publishing House.
Published 1990
Printed in the United States of America
ISBN 0-8100-0323-6

CONTENTS

ILLUSTRATIONS

This book is dedicated to my wife for all the love, encouragement and support she has given me and to our children who have filled our lives with joy.

INTRODUCTION

In *Kingdoms and Conquests* we will discuss the development and struggle for power between heathen nations and Israel in the Fertile Crescent during the years 931-586 B.C. We will see some of the intrigue, changes in power and atrocities so prevalent in those years. They are years that contain stories that come alive, if a person only gives them a chance. Unfortunately, most people are unfamiliar with them because the Old Testament today has basically become a closed book. It is questioned, doubted and attacked by historians and theologians alike; it is largely ignored by the man in the street.

The secular period of time with which this book deals and the dates given in the Bible are said to be irreconcilable in places. It is my two-fold hope that in reading *Kingdoms and Conquests* you will find your love and understanding for this period of Old Testament history heightened and that doubts or questions as to whether God's Word contains any mistakes will be done away with.

It is not my intention to offer an exhaustive study of the Old Testament nation of Israel. Instead, as you will find out, the history of Assyria and Syria receive more detailed treatment in some places than does the history of Israel and Judah. I have done this intentionally to try to build an overall view of how God used the events and the times to shape Old Testament history.

Because of the nature of this book — namely, that it treats the historical accounts of several nations — in some parts it was necessary to continue the history of several nations and then go back in time to see what was happening in another country during that same period of time. I trust this will not confuse the reader.

Death of Ahab (1 Kings 2:34-38)

1. THE STRUGGLE FOR POWER
931-797 B.C.

As we consider the development and struggle for power between the nations in the Fertile Crescent and the Children of Israel, one question has to be asked. How did it all begin? The answer really lies in the disappointing rule of King Solomon.

Solomon had been tremendously blessed by God. The Lord had given him riches, honor and, most importantly, a wise and understanding heart. Yet despite all of these blessings showered upon him by God, Solomon foolishly departed from following the Lord during his forty-year reign. He built shrines to the gods of his foreign wives and even worshiped them. There is good reason to believe that later in his life he repented, but the damage had already been done. Still, God, for the sake of Solomon's father David, permitted Solomon to finish out his life as the ruler of a united kingdom.

In judgment as well as in preparation for the future, God raised up three particular foes against him. One would be the future leader of Syria (also known as Aram); his name was Rezon. He escaped when David defeated the forces of Zobah; he then made his headquarters in Damascus, Syria. In time he developed into a continual foe of Solomon. The second foe of Solomon was Hadad the Edomite. He had escaped as a child, with the help of some Edomite officials, when Joab the commander of David's army destroyed all the men of Edom. The officials took him to Egypt, where he grew up and married the sister of the wife of Pharaoh.

1

Solomon's third enemy would eventually head the division of Israel into North and South. His name was Jeroboam. He was a gifted man whom Solomon himself had promoted over the house of Joseph. The Prophet Ahijah told Jeroboam that God would give him ten of the tribes of Israel because of the wickedness that Solomon had brought upon the land. Solomon therefore desired to kill Jeroboam, but Jeroboam escaped to Egypt, as 1 Kings 11:28-32 records:

> Now Jeroboam was a man of standing, and when Solomon saw how well the young man did his work, he put him in charge of the whole labor force of the house of Joseph. About that time Jeroboam was going out of Jerusalem, and Ahijah the prophet of Shiloh met him on the way, wearing a new cloak. The two of them were alone out in the country, and Ahijah took hold of the new cloak he was wearing and tore it into twelve pieces. Then he said to Jeroboam, "Take ten pieces for yourself, for this is what the LORD, the God of Israel, says: 'See, I am going to tear the kingdom out of Solomon's hand and give you ten tribes.
>
> But for the sake of my servant David and the city of Jerusalem, which I have chosen out of all the tribes of Israel, he will have one tribe.' "

When Solomon died in 931 B.C. the judgment that God had prepared came about through the foolishness of Rehoboam, the son of Solomon. The people said that they would follow him as their king if he would only lighten the burden that his father had laid upon them. Instead of listening to their plea, Rehoboam said that he would tax and treat them more harshly than his father had. That statement was all that Jeroboam needed. Quickly he moved the people to declare,

> What share do we have in David, what part in Jesse's son?
> To your tents, O Israel! Look after your own house, O David! (1 Kings 12:16)

In anger Rehoboam gathered 180,000 men to fight against Israel and bring them again into submission. God stopped the war before it started by saying through the prophet Shemaiah, "This is my doing."

The split into a divided monarchy became permanent as God declared it would be. The ten tribes that followed Jeroboam became known as Israel, and the tribe that followed Rehoboam became known as Judah. To insure the permanency of his position, Jeroboam initiated four changes in Israel:

1. He changed the place of worship from Jerusalem to Dan and Bethel so that the people would not become influenced by returning to Jerusalem every year.

2. He changed the symbols of worship to two golden calves.

3. He changed the religious calendar one month later for the celebrating of festivals.

4. When the priests objected and refused the changes, he sold the right to the priesthood for one bullock and seven rams.

Because of this the Bible says — twenty-one times! — that Jeroboam the son of Nadab made Israel sin.

The split gave Rezon the opportunity he needed to build Damascus into a formidable power without interference. Rehoboam died in 913 and was succeeded by his son Abijam as king of Judah. Abijam added to Syria's strong position with a tremendous victory over Jeroboam in which 500,000 Israelites were killed. This tremendous defeat forced Israel into a position of making alliances with other nations, Syria being the most important one.

Rezon was succeeded by Tabrimon and he was succeeded by his son Ben-Hadad I. With the latter we see the real beginning of interaction between Damascus on the one hand and Israel and Judah on the other. It was this Ben-Hadad I to whom Asa, the third king of Judah and the son of Abijam, sent tribute, requesting that he break his treaty with Baasha, son of Jeroboam, king of Israel, and attack him. Asa had brought a great revival into Judah that even reached into Israel. When Baasha saw that his subjects were being affected by this revival, he began to build at Ramah. This fortification was viewed by Asa as a threat for two reasons:

1. Politically, it becomes very uncomfortable to have your rival build a stronghold five miles from your capital.

2. Spiritually, the fortification of Ramah was Baasha's answer to Asa's great revival. It served as his iron bars which prevented defection among his subjects and dampened the spirit of Asa's reformation.

The appeal of Asa was successful. Baasha had to stop building Ramah to contend with Ben-Hadad, as 2 Chronicles 16:4-6 shows:

> Ben-Hadad agreed with King Asa and sent the commanders of his forces against the towns of Israel. They conquered Ijon, Dan, Abel Maim and all the store cities of Naphtali. When Baasha heard this, he stopped building Ramah and abandoned his work.
>
> Then King Asa brought all the men of Judah, and they carried away from Ramah the stones and timber Baasha had been using. With them he built up Geba and Mizpah.

About this time development and consolidation were taking place in Assyria under Tukulti Urta II. He was a vigorous leader, taking control over the desert tribes on the Tigris and Euphrates Rivers. Five campaigns are listed by D. D. Luckenbill in brief form, but the sixth campaign down the Tigris, across the Euphrates and up the Habur Valley is recounted in more detail.

4

After Tukulti Urta died, his son, Ashurnasirpal II, became King of Assyria. Throughout his reign he was a victorious ruler but extremely cruel. If ever a person had an exalted opinion of himself, he did. This is what he writes about himself:

> ... son of Tukulti-Urta, priest of Assur, who overcame all his enemies and fixed the bodies of his foes upon stakes; grandson of Adad-Nirari, the priest, the viceroy of the great gods, who brought about the overthrow of those that did not obey him and established his sway over all, the descendant of Assurdan, who freed [?] cities and founded temples. And now at the command of the great gods my sovereignty, my dominion, and my power are manifesting themselves: I am regal, I am lordly, I am exalted, I am mighty, I am honored, I am glorified, I am preeminent, I am powerful, I am valiant, I am lion-brave and I am heroic! [I], Ashurnasirpal, the mighty king, the king of Assyria, chosen of Sin, favorite of Anu, beloved of Adad, mighty one among the gods, I am a king mighty in battle, destroying cities and highlands, first in war, king of the four quarters [of the world], who had conquered his foes, destroyed all his enemies, king of all regions [of earth], of all princes, every one of them, the king who has trampled down all who were not submissive to him, and who has brought under his sway the totality of all people.[1]

He conquered the tribes of the middle Euphrates and extended Assyrian control from the Upper Sea to Babylon. In these victories he boasted about his brutalities. One city to feel and witness his cruelty was the city of Suru of Bit Halupe. Of his campaign against it, he states:

> I built a pillar over against his city gate, and I flayed all the chief men who had revolted, and I covered the pillar with their skins; some I walled up within the pillar, some I impaled upon the pillar on stakes, and others I bound to stakes round the pillar; many within the border of my own land I flayed, and I spread their skins upon the walls, and I cut off

5

the limbs of the officers, of the royal officers, who had rebelled. Ahiabab I took to Nineveh; I flayed him; I spread his skin upon the wall of Nineveh.[2]

When Hulai, the governor of Kinabu, tried to revolt, he was defeated and was flayed. Some of the survivors made a last stand at the city of Tela but were defeated and mutilated by Ashurnasirpal. He describes this, saying:

> From Kinabu I departed [and] to the city of Tela I drew near. The city was exceeding strong and was surrounded by three walls. The men trusted in their mighty walls and in their hosts, and did not embrace my feet. With battle and slaughter I stormed the city and captured it. Three thousand of their warriors I put to the sword; their spoil and their possessions, their cattle and their sheep I carried off. Many captives from among them I burned with fire, and many I took as living captives. From some I cut off their hands and their fingers [?]; of many I put out the eyes. I made one pillar of the living, and another of heads, and I bound their heads to posts [tree trunks] round about the city. Their young men and maidens I burned in the fire and it consumed them.[3]

His list goes on and on. Damascus and Israel were apparently bypassed, and with good reason. Damascus under Ben-Hadad I had become extremely powerful, while Israel now under Omri's leadership was growing in strength. Omri purchased the strategic hill of Samaria and made it his capital. So important was this move on Omri's part that the land was called the "land of Omri." He further strengthened his fortifications and offset Syria's dominance by making an alliance with Phoenicia, sealing it with the marriage of his son Ahab to Jezebel, the daughter of Ethball, King of the Sidonians.

It is quite interesting that there is no record of war between Omri and Ben-Hadad immediately. Indeed, it is rare that two powerhouses could exist in such close quarters without opposing one another. When this rarity does occur, there is generally a good reason. In this case the reason was quite obvious. Ashurnasirpal II was extending the Assyrian kingdom. He was a threat that had to be watched and feared. War between Syria and Israel would take place only if one or the other was greatly weakened and could be conquered without much loss.

The first nation to weaken was Israel, for God struck the land of Israel with three years of drought because of the wickedness of King Ahab. The drought was so severe that Ahab and Obediah went in search of grass to save the horses and mules so that all the animals would not be lost. When the drought ended by Elijah's prayer, what must Israel have looked like? If ever weakness had its grip on a nation, it had its grip on Israel. What better time to invade a land than after a national disaster like this. Not only were the resources of Israel drained, but morality was at a very low state. Ben-Hadad seized upon this golden opportunity around the year 857. He was tremendously confident of victory as can be seen in his demands of surrender.

> "Your silver and gold are mine, and the best of your wives and children are mine."
>
> The king of Israel answered, "Just as you say, my lord the king. I and all I have are yours."
>
> The messengers came again and said, "This is what Ben-Hadad says: 'I sent to demand your silver and gold, your wives and your children. But about this time tomorrow I am going to send my officials to search your palace and the houses of your officials. They will seize everything you value and carry it away.' " (1 Kings 20:3-6)

After this demand Ben-Hadad held a drinking party with thirty-two kings accompanying him. This last demand was more than Ahab could endure, so he prepared for war. Ahab's military strength was pathetic. He raised an army of only 7,232 men. It is no wonder that Ben-Hadad made such preposterous demands. God, however, intervened on Israel's behalf and Israel won. Well had Moses said, "How could one man chase a thousand, or two put ten thousand to flight, unless their Rock had sold them, unless the LORD had given them up? For their rock is not like our Rock, as even our enemies concede" (Deuteronomy 32:30,31). Israel's Rock, the true God, was able to overcome staggering odds to defeat the Syrians and achieve his purposes.

The next year Syria again attacked Israel, just as the Prophet Elijah had said they would. Because Syria had said, "Their gods are gods of the hills . . . not on the plains," God again made Israel victorious over staggering odds. As a result 127,000 footmen of Syria were slain and Ben-Hadad surrendered to Ahab.

The victory naturally gave back to Israel much of the strength and wealth it had lost in the drought. For Syria the effect was devastating and it could have resulted in the end of Syrian power, but Ahab had different ideas. He apparently saw Syria as a much-needed buffer between himself and Assyria.

Meanwhile, in Assyria, Ashurnasirpal II had died in 859. His son Shalmaneser III was now on the throne. In 857 he captured the city of Carchemish. About that same time a golden opportunity unfolded before his eyes. As we saw, Syria and Israel started fighting each other. How intriguing it must have seemed to him and how carefully he must have watched those two battles between Ahab and Ben-Hadad. Syria, as we noted, suffered greatly in the two battles.

In 853, because the forces of Assyria were getting ever closer, Syria and Israel united with nine other cities to fight Assyria at Karkar. Ahab supplied 2,000 chariots and 10,000 footmen. Ben-Hadad supplied 1,000 chariots and 20,000 footmen. Irhuleni of Hamath supplied 700 chariots. Although Assyria claimed victory, the extent of the claim could be disputed on three points:

1. Assyria did not continue on to Hamath.

2. Assyria waited until 849 before trying another invasion.

3. Ahab felt free enough from the Assyrian menace to break his alliance with Syria, for together with Jehoshaphat king of Judah he attacked Syria that same year. In this battle for Ramoth Gilead, not only were Ahab and Jehoshaphat defeated, but Ahab was also killed.

Ahab was succeeded by his son Ahaziah, who ruled from 853-852. During his reign Moab rebelled against Israel. When Ahaziah died in 852 he was succeeded by his brother Joram. It was most likely in his first year, 851, that he persuaded Jehoshaphat of Judah to join forces with him against Moab. They were joined by Edom and with the Prophet Elisha's help were victorious.

> He also sent this message to Jehoshaphat king of Judah: "The king of Moab has rebelled against me. Will you go with me to fight against Moab?"
>
> "I will go with you," he replied. "I am as you are, my people as your people, my horses as your horses."
>
> "By what route shall we attack?" he asked.
>
> "Through the Desert of Edom," he answered.
>
> So the king of Israel set out with the king of Judah and the king of Edom. After a roundabout march of seven days, the army had no more water for themselves or for the animals with them.
>
> "What!" exclaimed the king of Israel. "Has the LORD called us three kings together only to hand us over to Moab?"
>
> But Jehoshaphat asked, "Is there no prophet of the LORD here, that we may inquire of the LORD through him?"

9

> An officer of the king of Israel answered, "Elisha son of Shaphat is here. He used to pour water on the hands of Elijah."
>
> Jehoshaphat said, "The word of the LORD is with him." So the king of Israel and Jehoshaphat and the king of Edom went down to him. (2 Kings 3:7-12)

> ... and he said, "This is what the LORD says: Make this valley full of ditches. For this is what the LORD says: You will see neither wind nor rain, yet this valley will be filled with water, and you, your cattle and your other animals will drink. This is an easy thing in the eyes of the LORD; he will also hand Moab over to you." (2 Kings 3:16-18)

Around 849 the inhabitants of Ammon, Moab and Mt. Seir set off with the intended purpose of driving out the Israelites from the nation of Judah. The size of the migration was so large that Jehoshaphat knew he did not have the strength to fight and win. Therefore in a beautiful prayer he asked God for help. In answer to his prayer God granted him a victory without his having to fight.

> After this, the Moabites and Ammonites with some of the Meunites came to make war on Jehoshaphat.
>
> Some men came and told Jehoshaphat, "A vast army is coming against you from Edom, from the other side of the Sea. It is already in Hazazon Tamar" (that is, En Gedi). Alarmed, Jehoshaphat resolved to inquire of the LORD, and he proclaimed a fast for all Judah. The people of Judah came together to seek help from the LORD; indeed, they came from every town in Judah to seek him.
>
> Then Jehoshaphat stood up in the assembly of Judah and Jerusalem at the temple of the LORD in the front of the new courtyard and said:
>
> "O LORD, God of our fathers, are you not the God who is in heaven? You rule over all the kingdoms of the nations. Power and might are in your hand, and no one can withstand you. O our God, did you not drive out the inhabitants of this land before your people Israel and give it forever to the

descendants of Abraham your friend? They have lived in it and have built in it a sanctuary for your Name, saying, 'If calamity comes upon us, whether the sword of judgment, or plague or famine, we will stand in your presence before this temple that bears your Name and will cry out to you in our distress, and you will hear us and save us.'

"But now here are men from Ammon, Moab and Mount Seir, whose territory you would not allow Israel to invade when they came from Egypt; so they turned away from them and did not destroy them. See how they are repaying us by coming to drive us out of the possession you gave us as an inheritance. O our God, will you not judge them? For we have no power to face this vast army that is attacking us. We do not know what to do, but our eyes are upon you." (2 Chronicles 20:1-12)

Early in the morning they left for the Desert of Tekoa. As they set out, Jehoshaphat stood and said, "Listen to me, Judah and people of Jerusalem! Have faith in the LORD your God and you will be upheld; have faith in his prophets and you will be successful." After consulting the people, Jehoshaphat appointed men to sing to the LORD and to praise him for the splendor of his holiness as they went out at the head of the army, saying:
> "Give thanks to the LORD,
> for his love endures forever."

As they began to sing and praise, the LORD set ambushes against the men of Ammon and Moab and Mount Seir who were invading Judah, and they were defeated. The men of Ammon and Moab rose up against the men from Mount Seir to destroy and annihilate them. After they finished slaughtering the men from Seir, they helped to destroy one another.

When the men of Judah came to the place that overlooks the desert and looked toward the vast army, they saw only dead bodies lying on the ground; no one had escaped. So Jehoshaphat and his men went to carry off their plunder, and they found among them a great amount of equipment and clothing and also articles of value — more than they could take away. There was so much plunder that it took three days to collect it. (2 Chronicles 20:20-25)

The years 849, 848 and 845 again brought Assyria against Syria, for Shalmaneser attacked Ben-Hadad in those years. Ben-Hadad weathered these attacks. But in 843 he became sick and his general Hazael killed him and took the throne. Syria had suffered greatly in the wars against Assyria. And now in addition the usurper Hazael was on the throne.

What an opportunity for King Joram of Israel to recover Ramoth Gilead from Syrian control! Quickly he persuaded Ahaziah king of Judah to join him. Hazael, however, had apparently restored stability to Syria, for he was able to defeat the combined forces of Joram of Israel and Ahaziah of Judah. The attack brought about a number of changes. It instilled a burning hatred within Hazael toward Israel, since he had been attacked at such a crucial time. It also ushered in a change for Israel and Judah. Jehu, Joram's general, at the direction of a prophet of the Lord rebelled against King Joram and killed both him and Ahaziah king of Judah.

Shalmaneser saw all of this new unrest and attacked Syria again in 841 and 837. Jehu not only left Hazael to fight Assyria alone; he even sent tribute to Shalmaneser. Because of this the hatred that had begun in Hazael's heart toward Israel was inflamed all the more. Hazael suffered some tremendous losses in these battles. In the 841 battle he lost 1,121 chariots and 470 of his cavalry. In the 837 battle he lost four cities. He would surely have lost more, but fortunately for Hazael unrest had developed in the Assyrian Empire. Assurdaninapli, the son of Shalmaneser, nearly split the kingdom when he led a revolt of twenty-seven cities.

The years that followed (835-805), gave Hazael the breathing spell he needed to recover his strength. He was now free to take out all his built up frustration and anger. And take it out he did on the most natural and ready whipping post at hand — Israel. So thoroughly was his anger poured out on Israel that the Bible says he left to Jehoahaz, the son to Jehu, a mere fifty horsemen, ten chariots and ten thousand footmen. Hazael also defeated the Philistines and was ready to attack Jerusalem, but King Joash paid him off. Finally, in desperation, Jehoahaz, king of Israel prayed to the Lord for help. The Bible says of this:

> Then Jehoahaz sought the LORD's favor, and the LORD listened to him, for he saw how severely the king of Aram was oppressing Israel. The LORD provided a deliverer for Israel, and they escaped from the power of Aram. So the Israelites lived in their own homes as they had before. (2 Kings 13:4,5)

The Bible clearly states that God answered Jehoahaz's prayer by sending a deliverer. But who was that deliverer? Many historians have pointed to the three victories of Joash, or the great reign of Jeroboam II. Yet neither Joash, the son of Jehoahaz, nor Jeroboam II, his grandson, really fit the description of the deliverer whom God gave. The Bible strongly implies that the deliverer came in Jehoahaz's reign, as is seen in the following passage.

> But they did not turn away from the sins of the house of Jeroboam, which he had caused Israel to commit; they continued in them. Also, the Asherah pole remained standing in Samaria.
>
> Nothing had been left of the army of Jehoahaz except fifty horsemen, ten chariots and ten thousand foot soldiers, for the king of Aram had destroyed the rest and made them like the dust at threshing time.
>
> As for the other events of the reign of Jehoahaz, all he did and his achievements, are they not written in the book of the annals of the kings of Israel? (2 Kings 13:6-8)

13

The question as to the identity of the deliverer is not unanswerable, however, for one person in Assyria fits perfectly. That one is Adadnirari, the son of Shamsi Adad, the son of Shalmaneser III. The main reason Hazael was free to attack Israel between the years 835 and 805 was because of the unrest in the Assyrian kingdom at the end of the reign of Shalmaneser III, as indicated previously. This unrest also occupied most of Shamsi Adad's reign. It became his task to regain the Assyrian power and influence, in other words, to bring unity out of revolution. He speaks of this in the records of his reign:

> Where Assur-danin-apli, in the time of Shalmaneser, his father, acted wickedly bringing about sedition, rebellion [and] wicked plotting, caused the land to rise in revolt, prepared for war, brought the pearls of Assyria, north and south, to his side, and made bold speeches [?], brought the cities into the rebellion, and set his face to begin strife and battle . . . a total of twenty-seven cities, along with their fortifications, which had revolted against Shalmaneser, king of the four regions [of the world], my father, and those which had gone to the side of Assur-danin-apli — at the command of the great gods, my Lords, I brought [these into submission at my feet].[4]

Shamsi Adad made three campaigns against Babylon and Fort Der on the Elamite frontier. His reign was not especially long (823-810). If he had not had to deal with internal problems in the Assyrian realm, perhaps he would have extended the Assyrian kingdom even farther than his father had.

It was his good fortune to have married a very capable wife named Semiramis. When he died, she took over the royal throne of Assyria and held its power and authority from 810 to 805 until her son, Adadnirari III, was old enough to take over the throne.

When he took over the throne in 805, he showed his desire for conquest. From the records, it seems that he must have defeated Syria twice between 805 and 802, for there are two different records of the tribute he received from Hazael. In one record Hazael (known by the name Mari in the Assyrian records) paid him 100 talents of gold and 1,000 talents of silver. In another record Hazael paid him 20 talents of gold and 2,300 talents of silver.

> [To march against Aram] I gave the command. Mari [I shut up] in Damascus [his royal city]; 100 talents of gold, 1,000 talents of silver . . . I received.[5]

> Against Aram [Syria] I marched. Mari, king of Aram —in Damascus, his royal city, I shut him up. The terrifying splendor of Assur, his [probably error for, my] lord, over-whelmed him and he laid hold of my feet, he became my vassal [lit., did my service]; 2,300 talents of copper, 5,000 talents of iron, colored woolen and linen garments, an ivory bed, an ivory couch, inlaid and bejeweled [?], property and his goods, in immeasurable quantity, in Damascus, his royal city, in his palace I received.[6]

Adadnirari also claimed to have restored Israel to the position of a tributary, a position begun by Jehu, for he says that he brought Omri's land into submission:

> . . . Hatti, Amurru, in its totality, Tyre, Sidon, Humri [Omriland, Israel] Edom, Palastu, up to the great sea of the setting sun — I brought [these lands] in submission to my feet. Tribute and tax I imposed upon them.[7]

As was mentioned, Adadnirari was most likely the de-liverer God sent in answer to Jehoahaz's prayer. He indeed weakened Syria, but there is no indication that he took Damascus and made it part of his empire.

Later in Adadnirari's reign, for some reason Assyria seems to have fallen from active power. One of the last indications of Assyria's strength during his reign, is found in a stele from Rimah which says that Jehoash of Israel paid Adadnirari tribute, probably in the first year of his reign, about 797. This would also agree with the view that Adadnirari was the deliverer sent in answer to Jehoahaz's prayer. Jehoahaz was no longer completely under Hazael's hand. Instead, he was now under Adadnirari, as his son Jehoash would also be in the beginning of his reign.

2. THE SEESAW OF NATIONS
796-735 B.C.

The year 796 brought in a great deal of change. One of the most obvious changes took place in the nation of Judah. Judah's king for the past thirty-nine years had been Joash the son of Ahaziah. His reign is readily divisable into two periods, following the life and death of Jehoiada. During the years that Jehoiada the priest was alive, Joash followed the Lord and even repaired the temple. However, when Jehoiada died Joash turned away from the ways Jehoiada had taught him. Joash became so calloused that he even had Jehoiada's son stoned to death for declaring God's word. In judgment God brought Syria against Judah. The Bible records this in 2 Chronicles.

> After the death of Jehoiada, the officials of Judah came and paid homage to this king, and he listened to them. They abandoned the temple of the LORD, the God of their fathers, and worshiped Asherah poles and idols. Because of their guilt, God's anger came upon Judah and Jerusalem. Although the LORD sent prophets to the people to bring them back to him, and though they testified against them, they would not listen.
>
> Then the Spirit of God came upon Zechariah son of Jehoiada the priest. He stood before the people and said, "This is what God says: 'Why do you disobey the LORD's commands? You will not prosper. Because you have forsaken the LORD, he has forsaken you.'"
>
> But they plotted against him, and by order of the king they stoned him to death in the courtyard of the LORD's temple. King Joash did not remember the kindness Zechariah's father Jehoiada had shown him but killed his son, who said as

he lay dying, "May the LORD see this and call you to account."

At the turn of the year, the army of Aram marched against Joash; it invaded Judah and Jerusalem and killed all the leaders of the people. They sent all the plunder to their king in Damascus. Although the Aramean army had come with only a few men, the LORD delivered into their hands a much larger army. Because Judah had forsaken the LORD, the God of their fathers, judgment was executed on Joash. When the Arameans withdrew, they left Joash severely wounded. His officials conspired against him for murdering the son of Jehoiada the priest, and they killed him in his bed. So he died and was buried in the City of David, but not in the tombs of the kings. (2 Chronicles 24:17-25)

What is most interesting is that Syria came with a small army after fighting the Philistines in Gath. This could indicate one of two things:

1. At this time Assyria was inactive, giving Syria a chance to plunder another weaker country. Yet it would also show weakness in Syria, because the Syrians came with only a small army.

2. Assyria could attack at any time, so most of the Syrian army stayed home.

The first choice is the more likely. Assyria was quiet during this time, and Syria did not have the strength it once had. The impression one gets is that the two countries were both worn out.

Around 795 Ben-Hadad II, the son of Hazael, became the new king of Syria. Under him the balance of power continued to change. As was noted earlier, Adadnirari seemed to have faded into the background. Only when Assyria was idle was it safe for other nations to fight among themselves for power lest they become an easy prey.

The kingdoms that were now fighting for power were Israel, Hamath, Judah and a weakened Syria. The first to fall was Syria under King Ben-Hadad II. The king on the throne of Israel at this time was Jehoash, the son of Jehoahaz. It became his job to try to pick up the pieces his father Jehoahaz had left of the kingdom of Israel. In desperation he went to the Prophet Elisha who was on his death bed and asked for help.

> Now Elisha was suffering from the illness from which he died. Jehoash king of Israel went down to see him and wept over him. "My father! My father!" he cried. "The chariots and horsemen of Israel!"
>
> Elisha said, "Get a bow and some arrows," and he did so. "Take the bow in your hands," he said to the king of Israel. When he had taken it, Elisha put his hands on the king's hands.
>
> "Open the east window," he said, and he opened it. "Shoot!" Elisha said, and he shot. "The LORD's arrow of victory, the arrow of victory over Aram!" Elisha declared. "You will completely destroy the Arameans at Aphek."
>
> Then he said, "Take the arrows," and the king took them. Elisha told him, "Strike the ground." He struck it three times and stopped. The man of God was angry with him and said, "You should have struck the ground five or six times; then you would have defeated Aram and completely destroyed it. But now you will defeat it only three times." (2 Kings 13:14-19)

All came to pass as Elisha had said. Jehoash of Israel defeated Ben-Hadad II three times and recovered all the land Hazael had taken from his father. Syria was obviously hurting on its southern border. Unfortunately for Ben-Hadad II, things were not looking much better on the northern border. Zakir, king of Hamath was also crowned king over Luash in its capital city of Hazrek. (Luash is called Hatarikka in the Assyrian records.) Ben-Hadad II saw this union as a tremendous threat and determined to remove it. He tried to make an alliance with twelve or eighteen kings to attack Hazrek.

Zakir was victorious over the alliance headed by Ben-Hadad. Zakir further states that only seven kings joined Ben-Hadad. It seems his influence had all but disappeared. To celebrate this victory, Zakir strengthened himself and built cities. This victory was later recorded on what is called the Zakir stele about 773.

With this defeat in mind the words Elisha had declared simply shout out: "You should have struck the ground five or six times; then you would have defeated Aram and completely destroyed it. But now you will defeat it only three times" (2 Kings 13:19). Syria would have been finished for good, crushed on all sides, had Jehoash struck the ground five or six times.

Very little is known about the last few years of Ben-Hadad II of Syria. There is an awesome silence that follows his death around 770 and that lasts for almost twenty years. During this time there is no known king of Syria. Many do not know what to make of this lapse, but considered in its historical time slot, it is an amazing confirmation of biblical truth. The Bible says that Jeroboam II, the son of Jehoash became exceedingly powerful. Of all the kings of Israel he was the strongest and ruled over the largest territory. His boundaries reached the borders of Hamath as the Prophet Jonah had predicted.

This would necessitate total domination over Syria. With this in mind the silence in Syria is neither unexpected nor strange. The silence is broken in 753 when Rezin became king of Syria. The date of 753 is indeed striking for, as will be seen later, many events in Israel led up to the revival of Syria.

While this power struggle had been going on among Israel, Hamath and Syria, Judah also became involved in the picture. Judah's king was Amaziah, the "thistle king" of

Judah. His reign started well as God granted him a large victory over Edom. In preparation for this battle Amaziah had enlisted 100,000 men of Israel and paid them in advance. However, a prophet of God told him that God would not bless his efforts with Israel's men present. In the battle that followed Amaziah was totally victorious against Edom. However, in his absence problems developed. The 100,000 men of Israel that he had dismissed raided his land. Amaziah was now tormented by three evils:

1. Pride at having defeated Edom.
2. Sin, because after he had defeated Edom he worshiped the gods of Edom.
3. Indignation over the invasion of his country.

Therefore he challenged King Jehoash of Israel to fight against him. Jehoash responded by thoroughly insulting Amaziah. He said there was no comparison between them. Following the insult he advised Amaziah to remain at home. Amaziah should have taken the advice, for the battle cost him 600 feet of his wall, the temple treasury and hostages. Amaziah himself was taken captive (for how long, we are not told). This would have necessitated Uzziah's being placed on the throne as coregent and would explain the rather lengthy overlapping of their reigns (twenty-three years, 791-768). This battle most likely took place in the year 791. The Bible records the battle as follows:

> After Amaziah king of Judah consulted his advisers, he sent this challenge to Jehoash son of Jehoahaz, the son of Jehu, king of Israel: "Come, meet me face to face."
> But Jehoash king of Israel replied to Amaziah king of Judah: "A thistle in Lebanon sent a message to a cedar in Lebanon, 'Give your daughter to my son in marriage.' Then a wild beast in Lebanon came along and trampled the thistle underfoot. You say to yourself that you have defeated Edom, and now you are arrogant and proud. But stay at

home! Why ask for trouble and cause your own downfall and that of Judah also?"

Amaziah, however, would not listen, for God so worked that he might hand them over to Jehoash, because they sought the gods of Edom. So Jehoash king of Israel attacked. He and Amaziah king of Judah faced each other at Beth Shemesh in Judah. Judah was routed by Israel, and every man fled to his home. Jehoash king of Israel captured Amaziah king of Judah, the son of Joash, the son of Ahaziah, at Beth Shemesh. Then Jehoash brought him to Jerusalem and broke down the wall of Jerusalem from the Ephraim Gate to the Corner Gate — a section about six hundred feet long. He took all the gold and silver and all the articles found in the temple of God that had been in the care of Obed-Edom, together with the palace treasures and the hostages, and returned to Samaria. (2 Chronicles 25:17-24)

Finally, in judgment against Amaziah for having turned away from the Lord, God permitted a conspiracy to develop against him. He was killed and his son Uzziah became king in 768. Under the influence of Zechariah a prophet, Uzziah became exceedingly strong.

Meanwhile Assyria reached one of its lowest and most inactive points. The decline of Assyrian power had started in the latter half of Adadnirari III's reign. When Shalmaneser IV came to the throne in 782, he was unable to curb the deterioration of Assyria's might. Then in 773 one of the worst things happened that could happen to a nation struggling for stability. The king died. Worse yet, he died young and childless. What was going to happen to the nation? What internal strife there must have been in Assyria at this time! It may well have split the nation. Somehow, Ashurdan III became the next king. Yet many questions needed to be answered. Would Ashurdan III be able to unite the nation? Would he be able to reverse the downward trend of Assyria?

It is quite probably at this time, in 773, that Jonah came proclaiming, "Forty more days and Nineveh will be overturned" (Jonah 3:4). What a striking proclamation of judgment upon Assyria's capital city, and how well it would fit in with the decline that was taking place. The Assyrians had every reason to believe it. The general feeling of all nations toward her was a mixture of hatred and fear. If Zakir of Hamath, Jeroboam II of Israel and Uzziah of Judah united, Assyria could easily be destroyed.

God indeed works in marvelous ways. Assyria, that arrogant nation, was brought low so that it would see its helplessness and desperate need. When this was done God reached out in his infinite love and mercy and converted people by Jonah's preaching. Countless souls were saved and made heirs of heaven, souls that would otherwise have been lost for eternity.

Ashurdan III continued to reign until 755. He was succeeded by Ashurnirari, 754-745, another weak king. Ashurnirari's greatest claim to fame was the treaty he made with King Mati-ilu. This treaty came about as a result of a campaign Ashurnirari made against Arpad in the second year of his reign. In part of this treaty Ashurnirari compares Mati-ilu with a mutilated ram, a comparison which shows Assyria returning to its brutal state of mind.

> If Mati-ilu [sins] against this treaty [lit. oath of these words], [then] as this ram is being brought up from its flock, [a ram] which shall not return to its flock and shall not [again] go at the head of its flock, so on [his] part, shall Mati-ilu, together with his sons, his daughters, [his nobles], and the people of his land, . . . not return to his land. Before his land [he shall not go].
>
> This head is not the head of the ram, the head of Mati-ilu [it is], the head of his sons, of his nobles, of the people, of his land.

> This limb is not a limb of the ram; it is the limb of Mati-ilu,
> the limb of his sons, [of his nobles], of the people of his land,
> is it. If Mati-ilu sins against these [oaths], as the limb [of this
> ram] is torn off, so may the limb of Mati-ilu, the limb of his
> sons, [his nobles, of the people of his land] be torn off. . . .[8]

The treaty continues with other vicious curses on Mati-ilu, his family and land. Apparently Mati-ilu remained under this treaty for about three years. Then he successfully revolted.

Meanwhile, it seemed everything was going right for Israel and Judah. Under Jeroboam II and Uzziah, Israel and Judah together reached the peak of their strength. But all good things on this earth come to an end. For Israel it came in a hurry. Jeroboam II died later in 754 and with his death came the beginnings of the punishments prophesied by Amos upon Israel for its unfaithfulness.

> Hear this word the LORD has spoken against you, O people
> of Israel . . . :
> "You only have I chosen of all the families of the earth;
> therefore I will punish you for all your sins." (Amos 3:1,2)
> Therefore this is what the Sovereign LORD says: "An ene-
> my will overrun the land; he will pull down your strongholds
> and plunder your fortresses." (Amos 3:11)

Zachariah, the son of Jeroboam II became the next king of Israel. He reigned for only six months and then Shallum assassinated him. Shallum's rule was even shorter, only one month, and then Menahem assassinated him. The date for the beginning of Menahem's reign is 752. What internal dissension must have been present in Israel during the year 753! As would be expected control over Syria seems to have been lost almost immediately, for in 753 Rezin became king of Syria. Syria needed some time to strengthen itself and that time was given, as Israel was going downhill fast.

The only real centralized power left was Judah under Uzziah, now fifty-five years old and in the thirty-ninth year of his reign. Since there was no way of knowing how many more years he had left, it must have seemed prudent to establish his son, Jotham, on the throne as co-ruler of Judah. Perhaps the rapid decline and internal decentralization which followed Jeroboam's death hastened this political move. As it turned out, this foresight undoubtedly preserved the unity of Judah during the judgment that fell upon Uzziah two years later in 750.

By the year 750 Uzziah had ruled as a God-fearing king for forty-one years. Unfortunately he now desired a higher position. He wanted to burn incense to the Lord in the holy place, a rite reserved only for the priests who were descendants of Aaron. The high priest, Azariah, and eighty other priests tried to stop him. They told him that it was forbidden for him to do this, but instead of listening to them, he grew exceedingly angry. God quickly and decisively made his will known, for even while the king was still angry, he was turned into a leper. The second book of Chronicles records the results:

> When Azariah the chief priest and all the other priests looked at him, they saw that he had leprosy on his forehead, so they hurried him out. Indeed, he himself was eager to leave, because the LORD had afflicted him.
> King Uzziah had leprosy until the day he died. He lived in a separate house — leprous, and excluded from the temple of the LORD. Jotham his son had charge of the palace and governed the people of the land. (2 Chronicles 26:20,21)

As we noted before, his son had been made co-ruler two years earlier in 752. He, therefore, was in a position to assume the reins of power. His father Uzziah would still be recognized as the king of Judah in 743 when Pul defeated Jotham's forces, but it was a position in which he could not officially function. How true the words of Christ are, "For whoever exalts himself will be humbled" (Matthew 23:12).

In 744 a man destined for greatness usurped the throne in Assyria and brought the nation to power again. His name was Tiglath-Pileser III. In Israel he was known as Pul, probably his real name before he assumed the title of Tiglath-Pileser. In every aspect he was a fitting king for Assyria. His records are full of battles and atrocities. In his second year as king he boasted of the number of people he hung on stakes and he tells of how he cut the fingers off the captives he let go.

The third year of his reign was an extremely active one. His power was growing and had to be stopped. It would take a great coalition of power to prevent his total domination of the Fertile Crescent. By putting the different historical records together we can piece together the way it seems to have happened. Mati-ilu, Rezin, Sadurri of Urartus, Hiram of Tyre, Pisiris of Carchemish, Salmal of Melid and a few others joined in an attempt to curb Assyria. They were defeated and had to pay tribute to Assyria in Arpad. As a result of this defeat, Menahem king of Israel was sure that he was the next one marked for destruction. The very thought terrified him. He therefore took steps to prevent the seemingly inevitable and to retain his throne. He did this by going up to the city of Arpad and surrendering himself to the Assyrian king. Pul accepted this act of submission and returned Menahem to the throne of Israel. However, Pul extracted heavy tribute in return for not conquering Israel.

The news of Menahem's act of submission must have come as quite a shock to Uzziah. There was no real buffer between himself and Assyria. Uzziah therefore took steps to try to remove the danger of attack. Quickly he organized a large coalition of undefeated cities like Hamath and Luash

(Hatarikka), to take advantage of any momentary weakness in Assyria as a result of the recent warfare.

Unfortunately for him and his allies, there was no weakness and this coalition was also defeated. Many have found it strange that there is no mention of any further action against Uzziah personally by Pul. The reason normally given is that Uzziah died shortly afterwards — the date generally accepted at around 742 — before Pul could do anything to him. We do not go along with this reasoning, because we believe that Uzziah did not die in the year 742 B.C. but in 739. (In a later chapter we will discuss this important difference in dating and its significance for Old Testament chronology.) There are other good reasons why Pul did not inflict personal punishment on King Uzziah:

1. The army that Uzziah organized would be led by generals and not by himself, for he was sixty-four years old and a leper. Even if the whole army had been captured, he could not be because he simply wasn't there.

2. The other allied cities could be more easily punished because they were nearer Arpad, Pul's temporary headquarters. But to attack Judah would mean a long hard march with what had to be by now a tired and depleted army. Judah would have every advantage. Their King Uzziah was still the rallying point. The only strength Judah had lost was that part of its army which had been sent off to fight. The country itself remained far from being conquered.

3. Assyria remained strangely quiet for about six years. The silence is not broken by a punitive war on Judah. Instead, it is broken by unrest in Urartu. Perhaps Pul's victory was not as great as he boasted it was.

About a year after Menahem submitted to Pul in Arpad, he died. His son, Pekahiah, became the new king of Israel. Apparently he willingly carried on the pro-Assyrian policy started by his father. This policy was not received very well by the people. They were the ones who felt the brunt of Pul's financial demands. The feeling of resentment was growing rapidly. One reason it grew so strong may be that Assyria had indeed been weakened in its recent battles. Then in 739, only two years after Pekahiah became king, the resentment against Assyria broke into the open. Pekah, a very capable man, as the leader of the anti-Assyrian policy, killed Pekahiah and became king of Israel.

Very little is known of Pekah's earlier years other than that he served as a general under Pekahiah. Yet it is possible to read between the lines and get a little better understanding of him. As was said, he was a general under Pekahiah, apparently on the east side of the Jordan. However, he was no ordinary general as can be seen in how his reign is dated. He ruled from 752-732. Menahem ruled from 752-742; Pekahiah ruled from 741-739. Clearly, then, Pekah held enough of a commanding position to take control as a king when the opportunity arose. The situation was basically similar to Abner's relationship to Ishbosheth years earlier. Ishbosheth was only a figurehead, while Abner held the actual strength and power. He could have easily become king if he had desired it.

The timing of the assassination and the initiation of an anti-Assyrian policy could not have been better. Unrest in Urartu was growing and demanding more and more of Assyria's attention. Things finally got so bad by 737 that Pul had to begin a large campaign to stop the revolt.

This was exactly what Israel and Syria needed. While Assyria was busy with Urartu, Pekah made an alliance with Rezin of Syria, whom he had most likely known for many years due to his high position on the east side of Jordan. Pul remained occupied from 737-735 with crushing the revolt of Urartu. During that time the bonds between Rezin and Pekah became closer and stronger. Then in 735 they invaded Judah. The reason for this invasion has been long debated. There are basically two accepted explanations:

1. They invaded to force Judah to join them in their anti-Assyrian coalition.

2. They invaded to cripple Judah in event of a war against Assyria.

When these two explanations are examined, a common factor can be found in both. That is the presupposition that Judah was at this time pro-Assyrian, an idea for which there is no definite proof. The supposed proof most often given to support this view is that Ahaz, king of Judah, appealed to Pul for help. This type of proof stands on shaky ground. A man who is desperate will appeal anywhere he can for help. It doesn't matter whether he likes the one who can help him or not. For example, Asa appealed to Ben-Hadad I for help against Baasha. Should we therefore conclude that Asa was pro-Syria? If so, we have a problem because Baasha and Ben-Hadad I had a mutual treaty and Asa had to bribe Ben-Hadad to break it.

There is another explanation for this invasion that is both simple and scriptural, but has been overlooked. As noted, Pul was off on a campaign from 737-735. During this time, in Assyria's absence, the forces of Israel and Syria were able to grow. As their strength grew, so did their desire for some rich plunder which would in turn increase their power. Because Assyria could return, whatever nation they plundered would have to be weak or in a disorganized condition. This would be necessary to insure a quick victory with minimal loss.

In 735, while Assyria was still occupied, such an opportunity offered itself to them. Judah appeared ripe for the picking. It was torn apart by internal dissension between the godly followers of Jotham and the ungodly followers of

Ahaz. Things seemed to have come to a head in 736 as can be seen by comparing the reigns and dates given to Jotham and Ahaz. According to 2 Kings 15:30 Jotham ruled for twenty years (752-732), but 2 Kings 15:33 says that Jotham ruled for sixteen years, (752-736). In 2 Kings 16:1 it says that Ahaz began to reign in Pekah's seventeenth year (735). Therefore Ahaz's first year of full power would be 735.

> Then Hoshea son of Elah conspired against Pekah son of Remaliah. He attacked and assassinated him, and then succeeded him as king in the twentieth year of Jotham son of Uzziah.
>
> He was twenty-five years old when he became king, and he reigned in Jerusalem sixteen years. His mother's name was Jerusha daughter of Zadok.
>
> In the seventeenth year of Pekah son of Remaliah, Ahaz son of Jotham king of Judah began to reign. (2 Kings 15:30,33; 16:1)

When these dates are all put together, it is quite interesting that Ahaz quite evidently took control of the throne even though his father was still alive. Perhaps there is a reason in the Bible that his name is recorded for us as Ahaz and not Jehoahaz as it is found in the Assyrian records. Ahaz means Possessor; Jehoahaz means Possessor of Jehovah. Ahaz possessed the throne but not Jehovah. The spiritual condition in Judah had grown worse and worse with Ahaz's rise in power. Finally, when he had achieved control and possessed the throne, God showed him that he, the Lord, was in control. In 735 God moved Pekah and Rezin to see the internal problems in Judah as an invitation to strike. And strike they did.

The plan was simple. Syria would attack from the south and come up while Israel would attack from the north and come down. Judah would have to surrender. They could then put Tabiel, a Phoenician, on the Judean throne to insure cooperation and tribute. One of the first great victories went to Rezin. He conquered the seaport of Elath on the Gulf of Akabah, drove out the Jews and made it a Syrian port city. From here he would march north toward Jerusalem. On this march he would conquer whoever opposed him. Meanwhile, Israel under Pekah was defeating Judah in the north and heading south toward Jerusalem. The losses inflicted on Judah were staggering. In one day Pekah's forces slew 120,000 men of Judah. The king's son Maaseiah, Azrikam the officer of his house and Elkanah, who was next to the king, were also killed. Judah was later plundered and 200,000 captives were deported by the army of Israel.

Fortunately for Judah, Oded, a prophet of the Lord, convicted the people of Israel of their heartless sins against their brothers from Judah. Fearing God's wrath, the Israelite armies restored the captives and spoils to Judah. What happened to those carried off by Syria is unknown.

When Edom and the Philistines saw how helpless the great power of Judah had become under Ahaz, they too rose up and fought against her. Ahaz therefore could do nothing but remain within the fortifications of Jerusalem. It was clear that something had to be done. Help had to be procured. Isaiah, the great prophet of God, came with a tremendous promise of deliverance but Ahaz in mock humility refused it. Instead of relying on God he took the matter into his own hands and sent a message to Pul to come and deliver him out of the hand of Israel and Syria.

There was no doubt in Rezin's or Pekah's mind that they would have to contend with Assyria. There was no time to lose in trying to take Jerusalem by siege. Their plans for acquiring booty and power were fulfilled. The only plan that was not fulfilled was the establishment of Tabiel on the throne of Judah.

31

Israelite Warriors

3. ASSYRIA THE CONQUEROR
734-705 B.C.

In the year 734 B.C. Assyria responded to the pleas of Ahaz for help. The revolts which had occupied Pul's time and energy had been crushed. He was therefore free to concentrate on the coalition of Pekah and Rezin from 734-732.

In the Assyrian records these years are lumped together with other victorious years of Pul's reign. Because of this it is quite difficult to pinpoint just what happened in what year. It is also difficult to lay out his strategy and the results it had. The following is an attempt to explain his invasion.

Pul had no desire or intention of meeting a unified coalition of Pekah and Rezin so he took steps to avoid such a confrontation. Instead of attacking Damascus (which would seem like the most obvious place to begin), he avoided it and passed by to the south of it. He was now in what would seem a most uncomfortable position — Syria on one side, Israel on the other. Yet this move was so unexpected that Israel was taken by surprise. The Israelite army had counted on going up to aid Syria, not on being the first one attacked. Pul quickly overran the cities of Dan and Naphtali, as 2 Kings 15 shows:

> In the time of Pekah king of Israel, Tiglath-Pileser king of Assyria came and took Ijon, Abel Beth Maacah, Janoah, Kedesh and Hazor. He took Gilead and Galilee, including all the land of Naphtali, and deported the people to Assyria. (2 Kings 15:29)

From there he continued down the Mediterranean coast and defeated the Philistines. Once in Gaza, he set up temporary headquarters and erected a statue of himself. Most likely at this time he also met with Ahaz and received necessary supplies and reinforcements. In 733 he marched from Gaza and again took Israel and Damascus by surprise. The most obvious place to attack was Samaria, the capital of Israel. Instead, he passed by it and went straight up to Damascus. The fact that he could pass so close to the capital of Samaria showed that he had little to fear from Israel. Pul now had the time he needed for a prolonged siege of Damascus without Israel, the Philistines or Egypt interfering. The siege was long and hard. It began in 733 and it ended with the complete destruction of Damascus in 732. Rezin, as would be expected, was killed and the inhabitants were deported to Kir as the Prophet Amos had foretold.

> This is what the LORD says: "For three sins of Damascus, even for four, I will not turn back my wrath. Because she has threshed Gilead with sledges having iron teeth, I will send fire upon the house of Hazael that will consume the fortresses of Ben-Hadad. I will break down the gate of Damascus; I will destroy the king who is in the Vally of Aven and the one who holds the scepter in Beth Eden. The people of Aram will go into exile to Kir." (Amos 1:3-5)

Although won by Assyria, this battle seems to have been a costly one, for Pul settled for a political victory over Israel instead of a complete military one. With Pul's support, Hoshea rallied Israel behind himself and slew Pekah to become the last king of Israel. Pul records the events as follows:

> This land of Bit-Humria ... all of its people, together with their goods, I carried off to Assyria. Pakaha, their king, they deposed and I placed Ausi'[Hoshea] over them as king. Ten talents of gold and [?] 127 talents of silver as their tribute I received from them, and to Assyria I carried them.[9]

After the defeat of Damascus and the ascent of Hoshea to the throne of Israel, King Ahaz of Judah quickly made a trip to Damascus to meet with Pul. While in Damascus he saw an altar that Pul had erected to the god Asshur. Because of the beauty of the altar and because he wanted to demonstrate his loyalty to Assyria, Ahaz had Urijah the priest duplicate it for him. This replica was then placed in the temple.

With this altar Ahaz changed the religious ceremonies of the temple. He ordered that all morning and evening meal offerings, kings' and peoples' offerings, drink offerings and all sprinkling of blood be done on it in total disregard of what God had established. He also had Jehovah's altar moved off to the side and out of the way, just as he had moved God off to the side and out of his life.

In righteous retribution four years later, in 728, God removed Ahaz from the earth. He was furthermore denied burial in the tombs of the kings.

With his victory over Damascus, Pul continued to expand his kingdom. Merodach-Baladan, called the king of the sea-land, submitted to the Assyrians around 730. Pul records that the tribute he paid was immense. Assyria also overran the kingdom of the Medes and carried off 65,000 people along with their possessions and animals. Their cities were burned and destroyed with typical Assyrian efficiency.

From the time Hoshea came to the throne of Israel in 732, Assyria received its required tribute from him. As these demands became harder to meet, the inclination to rebel started to grow. These feelings increased with the promise of help from So, a petty king of Egypt.

When Pul died in 727, Israel took the opportunity to rebel and cease paying tribute. Pul's son Shalmaneser V was now king. He was not about to tolerate such a rebellious act, and under threat of punishment Israel relented and paid its tribute. Hoshea, however, still continued his relation with So of Egypt. Therefore, in 725 Shalmaneser imprisoned Hoshea and besieged Samaria. The siege lasted three years. Finally, Samaria fell in 723.

There is a question whether Shalmaneser or Sargon his brother actually completed the siege and took the city. Shalmaneser clearly is the king who laid siege to Samaria, but there is no direct statement that he took it. Sargon, his general and the next king of Assyria, claimed that he took the city in his first year and deported its inhabitants.

> I besieged and captured Samaria, carrying off 27,000 of the people who dwelt therein. Fifty chariots I gathered from among them. I caused them to take their [the deported inhabitants'] portion. I set my officers over them and imposed upon them the tribute of the former king.[10]

There is a problem in Sargon's claim of having taken the city of Samaria. He would have taken it in the year 722-721, not 723-722. This would necessitate a longer siege than the Bible has evidence for in two references:

1. The beginning of the three-year siege was in the seventh year of Hoshea and the city was taken in his ninth year, 725-723.

2. The three-year siege began in the fourth year of Hezekiah and ended in his sixth year, 725-723.

> Shalmaneser king of Assyria came up to attack Hoshea, who had been Shalmaneser's vassal and had paid him tribute. But the king of Assyria discovered that Hoshea was a traitor, for he had sent envoys to So king of Egypt, and he no longer paid tribute to the king of Assyria, as he had done year by year. Therefore Shalmaneser seized him and put him in prison. The king of Assyria invaded the

entire land, marched against Samaria and laid siege to it for three years. In the ninth year of Hoshea, the king of Assyria captured Samaria and deported the Israelites to Assyria. He settled them in Halah, in Gozan on the Habor River and in the towns of the Medes. (2 Kings 17:3-6)

In King Hezekiah's fourth year, which was the seventh year of Hoshea son of Elah king of Israel, Shalmaneser king of Assyria marched against Samaria and laid siege to it. At the end of three years the Assyrians took it. So Samaria was captured in Hezekiah's sixth year, which was the ninth year of Hoshea king of Israel. (2 Kings 18:9,10)

It therefore seems more biblically correct to credit the taking of Samaria to Shalmaneser. What then should be done with Sargon's great claim? There is a way that Sargon could legitimately claim the victory for himself. When a general in charge of the army conquered a city and the king was not there, he could get credit for it instead of the king. This was why Joab appealed to David to come to Rabbah lest he (Joab) take the city and it be credited to him.

Joab then sent messengers to David, saying, "I have fought against Rabbah and taken its water supply. Now muster the rest of the troops and besiege the city and capture it. Otherwise I will take the city, and it will be named after me." (2 Samuel 12:27,28)

With this in mind and noting the fact that Shalmaneser died shortly after the fall of Samaria, we would naturally expect Sargon to make such a claim. Regardless of whether Sargon was king at the time he took the city or not, he was definitely the king who deported Samaria, and he did it in his first year as king.

During Shalmaneser and Sargon's preoccupation with Samaria, Merodach-Baladan had enough time to expand his territorial control. In 722 he became the king of Babylon.

Once Sargon completed the deportation of Samaria in 722, he claimed to have defeated Merodach-Baladan and deported many of the people and possessions.

> [Merodach-Baladan, king of Chaldea], who exercised the kingship over Babylon against the will of the gods . . . the people, together with their possessions, I snatched away. . . . [In the land] of Hatti [Syria] I settled [them].[11]

This claim of victory can be questioned not only because of its brevity, but also because Merodach-Baladan retained enough power to remain the king of Babylon. What was it that prevented the Assyrians from obtaining total victory? There seem to be two reasons.

1. As will be seen later, Merodach-Baladan had the tremendous ability to avoid capture by going into the marshlands of the Persian Gulf. To dislodge him from such a place would take a lot of time, and time was one thing Sargon did not have. He did not have it because of reason number 2.

2. Ilu bi di, a pretender to the throne of Hamath, caused a spirit of revolt to grow in Sargon's absence at Babylon. This revolt took place in Sargon's second year. The spirit of revolt grew quickly under Ilu bi di, enabling him to assemble a large coalition to oppose Assyria. As unbelievable as it seems, Samaria and Syria also joined the rebellion. Their forces were defeated at Karkar. Karkar was burned with fire, Ilu bi di was flayed and 9,000 people were carried off with their possessions.

> Il'u-bi'di of Hamath — a camp-follower with no claim to the throne, an evil Hittite, who was plotting in his heart to become king of Hamath, and causing the cities of Arpadda, Simirra, Damascus and Samaria to revolt against me — had unified them and prepared for battle. I mustered the masses of Assur's troops and at Karkar, his favorite city, I besieged and captured him, together with his warriors.

Karkar I burned with fire. Him I flayed. In the midst of
those cities I slew the rebels, I established harmony. Two
hundred chariots, six hundred cavalry, I gathered from
among the people of Hamath and added them to my royal
equipment [armament].[12]

While all this was going on, Judah was divinely spared.
Ahaz, as was noted previously, died in 728. His son, Hezekiah, succeeded him as king of Judah. In his first year he
reopened the doors of the temple, gathered together the
priests and Levites, had the temple cleared and sanctified,
and commanded offerings to be sacrificed on the altar of the
Lord. All this was done with one thing in mind, to return to
the covenant relationship and the blessings contained in it.

It was most likely in 726, his third year, that he rebelled
against the Assyrians and refused to serve them. In this year
he also defeated the Philistines as far as Gaza. Pul died in
727, so the time for a rebellion was well chosen. Shalmaneser, Pul's successor, had many such rebellions to contend
with. We have seen that Israel under Hoshea also rebelled at
this time; but Israel's capital was placed under siege in 725
and fell in 723. The short reign of Shalmaneser was indeed a
blessing for Judah. Perhaps the main reason for Shalmaneser's brief reign was that he had marked Judah as his
next target, a target now returning to God's protecting hand
under King Hezekiah. Sargon, Shalmaneser's successor,
was kept so busy trying to retain control over the empire
that to attack Judah was simply out of the question.

What a beautiful position Judah was now occupying! The
country was again receiving God's blessings in battle, econ-
omy and worship. Then, in 715, it seemed a great tragedy
was about to strike. Hezekiah became very ill and God
instructed the Prophet Isaiah to tell him to set his house in
order, for he was going to die. What a blow, to lose such a

39

leader in the prime of his life! Imagine the feelings that Isaiah was experiencing. He had tried to work with Ahaz, Hezekiah's father, without success. How thrilled he must have been to see the reforms of Hezekiah! It was undoubtedly with a heavy heart that in obedience to God's command he went and delivered his message of death.

Hezekiah responded to this message by turning toward the wall and praying to the Lord. While he was still praying and before Isaiah had gone out of the middle court, God told Isaiah to return to Hezekiah and tell him that fifteen years would be added to his life. What joy must have filled Isaiah's heart as he hurried back to deliver this message of life! To confirm this promise God granted Hezekiah the miracle of the shadow going backward ten steps.

> Hezekiah had asked Isaiah, "What will be the sign that the LORD will heal me and that I will go up to the temple of the LORD on the third day from now?"
>
> Isaiah answered, "This is the LORD's sign that the LORD will do what he has promised: Shall the shadow go forward ten steps, or shall it go back ten steps?"
>
> "It is a simple matter for the shadow to go forward ten steps," said Hezekiah. "Rather, have it go back ten steps."
>
> Then the prophet Isaiah called upon the LORD, and the LORD made the shadow go back the ten steps it had gone down on the stairway of Ahaz. (2 Kings 20:8-11)

This sign quickly became famous, for it contained a message. Judah's history had revolved around special signs and examples of God's active power, demonstrations of divine power that other nations often talked about. Now here was a new one — one that showed God was again active amid his people. Other nations, beware! The news of the miracle even reached Babylon. In response, Merodach-Baladan, king of Babylon, sent a delegation 600 miles to Jerusalem. The Bible gives the reason for this delegation. They came to ask about the miracle that was done in the land. Did the God of Israel really control the sun and the shadow cast from it? Was the reason for this miracle solely a demonstration of God's favor and care for Hezekiah as they had heard?

> It was Hezekiah who blocked the upper outlet of the Gihon spring and channeled the water down to the west side of the City of David. He succeeded in everything he undertook. But when envoys were sent by the rulers of Babylon to ask him about the miraculous sign that had occurred in the land, God left him to test him and to know everything that was in his heart. (2 Chronicles 32:30,31)

What an opportunity Hezekiah had to show the glories of his God! He could explain that the Lord alone is the true God, that all other gods are idols and the works of men's hands. He could explain why his country was the recipient of such divine care in the light of the Messianic promise of God. Instead, his pride got in the way. Hezekiah pointed out that *he* indeed possessed the blessings of God. To prove his claim, he showed them all of his wealth and power. The Bible sums up Hezekiah's foolishness when it says:

> But Hezekiah's heart was proud and he did not respond to the kindness shown him. (2 Chronicles 32:25)

As soon as the delegation departed, Isaiah asked Hezekiah what he had shown to them. When Isaiah heard that he showed them all his wealth, he announced God's judgment. The judgment was plain and clear. It was a judgment that would fall in all of its force upon Judah a little over 100 years later.

> Then Isaiah said to Hezekiah, "Hear the word of the LORD: The time will surely come when everything in your palace, and all that your fathers have stored up until this day, will be carried off to Babylon. Nothing will be left, says the LORD." (2 Kings 20:16,17)

A year or two after the delegation from Babylon visited Judah, Sargon now in his eleventh year found it necessary to deal with Azuru, king of Ashdod. Azuru not only refused to pay tribute, but became openly hostile to Assyria. Sargon removed him as king and replaced him with Ahimita, Azuru's brother. But the people hated Ahimita and they deposed him and replaced him with Iamani. Sargon was quick to respond. Ashdod and Gath were besieged and captured. In his haste to flee to Ethiopia Iamani left his wife, sons and daughters to be captured.

It was at this time with Assyria so close at hand that God told Isaiah to walk without his outer garment and barefoot for three years as a picturesque sign not to depend on Egypt or Ethiopia for help against Assyria. Their help was in the Lord. As for Egypt and Ethiopia, they would be led away as captives. Isaiah recorded this in chapter 20:

> In the year that the supreme commander, sent by Sargon king of Assyria, came to Ashdod and attacked and captured it — at that time the LORD spoke through Isaiah son of Amoz. He said to him, "Take off the sackcloth from your body and the sandals from your feet." And he did so, going around stripped and barefoot.
>
> Then the LORD said, "Just as my servant Isaiah has gone stripped and barefoot for three years, as a sign and portent against Egypt and Cush, so the king of Assyria will lead away stripped and barefoot the Egyptian captives and Cushite exiles, young and old, with buttocks bared — to Egypt's shame. Those who trusted in Cush and boasted in Egypt will be afraid and put to shame. In that day the people who live on this coast will say, 'See what has happened to those we relied on, those we fled to for help and deliverance from the king of Assyria! How then can we escape?' " (Isaiah 20:1-6)

The false security of Ethiopia as an ally was clearly shown, when later that same year the king of Ethiopia brought Iamani, bound in fetters and shackles, and turned him over to Sargon. His flight to Ethiopia had been in vain, for the king of Ethiopia turned him over to Sargon to show his good will toward Assyria.

> The king of Mcluhha [Ethiopia], who [dwelt] in the midst of . . . an inapproachable region, whose fathers since the far-off days of the moon god's time had not sent messengers to the kings my fathers, to bring their greetings, [that the Ethiopian king] heard from afar of the might of Assur, Nabu and Marduk and the terrifying splendor of my royalty over-powered him and fright overcame [lit., was poured upon] him, in fetters, shackles and bonds of iron, he cast him [the fugitive Iamani]. And they brought him before me into Assyria, after a most difficult journey.[13]

Sargon was indeed very near Judah and in a position from which he could attack. All he needed was a little break from countries continually trying to revolt against him and he could then concentrate on expanding his kingdom. Fortunately for Judah, Sargon was not to get any such break. The next year, 710, Merodach-Baladan again organized a rebellion against Assyria, probably using Assyria's absence in Ashdod as a stepping stone. The desert and marshland tribes joined Merodach-Baladan's rebellion.

The alliance was powerful enough that it took two years for the Assyrians to defeat it. After the first year Merodach-Baladan was forced to retreat and prepare new fortifications. He went to Dur Iakin, not far from Babylon and near the Euphrates River. It had become painfully clear that his forces could not withstand the Assyrian attack, so he devised some ingenious strategy to control the number of Assyrians that could attack at once. He did this by making a moat three hundred feet wide and thirteen and a half feet deep which he filled with water. To further control the areas of battle, he cut a channel from the Euphrates and flooded the plain where the battles were fought. In various high spots he established his defenses.

The strategy was good but the Assyrians were still victorious. Sargon claims to have taken Dur Iakin and to have gathered together Merodach-Baladan, his wife, his sons, his daughter, all of his riches, the rest of the rebellious people and counted them all as spoil. The extent of this claim can be questioned for two reasons.

1. There is no direct mention of punishment being inflicted on Merodach-Baladan, as was done to others who dared to oppose Sargon.

2. Merodach-Baladan retained much of his influence and power as a local ruler, though he made no more open rebellion against Assyria until Sargon died four years later in 705.

4. SUSTAINED STRENGTH AND DEPORTATIONS
705-670 B.C.

Sargon died in 705 B.C. and was succeeded by Sennacherib. Merodach-Baladan saw this as his opportunity to lead another rebellion against Assyria and again become the king of Babylon. Under his leadership a tremendous alliance was formed. Into this alliance he brought the Elamites, the area of Akkad, the area of Sumer and the plain of Kish.

When Sennacherib heard of the rebellion he became furious. The great Assyrian army was quickly mobilized to crush Merodach-Baladan. Sennacherib was so overtaken by anger that he foolishly decided to send his captains and governors ahead of the main army, after Merodach-Baladan into the plain of Kish. This decision resulted in the loss of his captains and governors. The news of the defeat was brought to Sennacherib when he reached the city of Kutha, where Merodach-Baladan had previously established his first line of defense. In total frustration and anger he attacked and defeated the fortified city of Kutha. With Kutha now out of the way he headed toward Kish to punish Merodach-Baladan and the rest of his alliance.

Sennacherib was totally victorious, but Merodach-Baladan again escaped by fleeing into the marshland of the Persian Gulf. For five days Sennacherib forced his army to search the swamps in an attempt to locate his hiding place, finally quitting without success. To curb his disappointment in Merodach-Baladan's escape, he tells of the joy he felt in plundering the treasures of Babylon and taking over its throne:

> In joy of heart and with a radiant face I hastened to Babylon and entered the palace of Merodach-Baladan, to take charge of the property and goods therein. I opened his treasure-house, gold, silver, vessels of gold and silver, precious stones, beds, house chairs, palanquins, his royal standards whose inlay was of gold and silver, all kinds of property and goods, and without number — an enormous treasure — his wife, his harem, his slave girls, his officials, his nobles, his courtiers, the male and female musicians, the palace slaves, who gladdened his princely mind, all of the artisans, as many as there were, his palace menials — these I brought forth and counted as spoil.
>
> I hurried after him, sent my warriors to Guzummsnu, into the midst of the swamps and marshes and they searched for him for five days, but his hiding place was not found.[14]

In his second campaign Sennacherib defeated the Kassites. This victory stabilized his reign in the southeastern part of his realm. At the end of this campaign he became the first Assyrian king to extend his yoke over the Medes. With the southeastern and eastern part of his kingdom now under control, he looked to the west and southwestern areas for continued expansion.

Around 702 Sennacherib began his third campaign. The first country to feel his might was Syria. From there he attacked Sidon and continued down the coastline of the Mediterranean Sea, defeating everything in front of him. In an effort to hold off the Assyrians the coastal city of Ekron enlisted the help of Egypt, but Sennacherib was still victorious. Not even the help of Egypt and Ethiopia could halt the Assyrian march. Ekron was punished severely for daring to make an alliance against Assyria. Their nobles and governors were hung on stakes around the city and many of the people were deported. It appeared that Sennacherib's third campaign would end in total success.

One great obstacle remained and that was Jerusalem under King Hezekiah. Sennacherib demanded his submission. Forty-six cities of Judah had already fallen to this Assyrian king. In submission Hezekiah sent him an apology for his rebellious actions and paid thirty talents of gold and three hundred talents of silver. It was probably along with this payment that Padi, the deposed king of Ekron was released and reestablished on the throne of Ekron. Padi had been faithful to his Assyrian overlords until he was bound in chains and delivered to Hezekiah, probably in Hezekiah's victorious third year. When Sennacherib saw how easily Hezekiah yielded to him, he wanted more. In order to satisfy this desire he sent his Tartan, second in rank, his Rabsaris, chief eunuch, and his Rabshakeh, the chief officer, to promote rebellion in the city of Jerusalem. It was hoped this would remove the necessity of a long siege. To instigate this rebellion Sennacherib's Rabshakeh used six major arguments.

> 1. The field commander said to them, "Tell Hezekiah: 'This is what the great king, the king of Assyria, says: On what are you basing this confidence of yours? You say you have strategy and military strength — but you speak only empty words. On whom are you depending, that you rebel against me? Look now, you are depending on Egypt, that splintered reed of a staff, which pierces a man's hand and wounds him if he leans on it! Such is Pharaoh king of Egypt to all who depend on him.' " (2 Kings 18:19-22)

Even though Hezekiah was not trusting in Egypt this argument would instill in many a feeling of despair. The inhabitants of Jerusalem knew all too well what had just happened to Ekron. Egypt and Ethiopia had not been able to save Ekron. How then could Jerusalem be saved?

> 2. "And if you say to me, 'We are depending on the LORD our God'" — isn't he the one whose high places and altars Hezekiah removed, saying to Judah and Jerusalem, 'You must worship before this altar in Jerusalem'?" (2 Kings 18:22)

In this argument Rabshakeh showed a complete lack of understanding of the Jewish religious services and concept of Jehovah as God by equating them with all religious worship.

> 3. "Come now, make a bargain with my master, the king of Assyria: I will give you two thousand horses — if you can put riders on them! How can you repulse one officer of the least of my master's officials, even though you are depending on Egypt for chariots and horsemen?" (2 Kings 18:23,24)

In sheer mockery an offer is given to provide horses so that they can fight. The major point was this: The Assyrian army is exceedingly powerful. Even if we helped you, you could not do a thing against us. How much less can you expect with Egypt's help?

> 4. "Furthermore, have I come to attack and destroy this place without word from the LORD? The LORD himself told me to march against this country and destroy it." (2 Kings 18:25)

This argument hit a nerve and in response the delegation from Hezekiah made a request:

> Then Eliakim son of Hilkiah, and Shebna and Joah said to the field commander, "Please speak to your servants in Aramaic, since we understand it. Don't speak to us in Hebrew in the hearing of the people on the wall." (2 Kings 18:26)

What was this nerve that was struck in the hearts of that delegation and perhaps in the hearts of the Jews in Jerusalem? The answer lies in an event that had taken place about 35 years earlier, an event through which many had lived and undoubtedly still talked about in hushed tones. Isaiah had been commanded by God to take his son Shear-jashub to the same spot on which the Assyrian delegation was now standing. He was to make an offer to King Ahaz —any miracle Ahaz asked for God would carry out in order to demonstrate that Ahaz had nothing to fear from his enemies Pekah and Rezin. As we noted earlier, in mock humility Ahaz said he would not tempt the Lord. Isaiah in frustration responded: Then Isaiah said, "Hear now, you house of David! Is it not enough to try the patience of men? Will you try the patience of my God also?" (Isaiah 7:13) Then Isaiah went on to pronounce this judgment:

> The LORD will bring on you and on your people and on the house of your father a time unlike any since Ephraim broke away from Judah — he will bring the king of Assyria.
> In that day the LORD will whistle for flies from the distant streams of Egypt and for bees from the land of Assyria. They will all come and settle in the steep ravines and in the crevices in the rocks, on all the thornbushes and at all the water holes. In that day the Lord will use a razor hired from beyond the River — the king of Assyria — to shave your head and the hair of your legs, to take off your beards also. (Isaiah 7:17-20)

Isaiah had clearly foretold that Assyria was going to wreak havoc on Judah. Now the Assyrians were standing in the same place where this judgment had been pronounced! It was no wonder that the delegation from Hezekiah did not want the people to hear any more. Apparently they did not see the significance of the name Shear-Jashub (meaning, "a remnant shall return") as it is used in Isaiah 10:

> In that day the remnant of Israel, the survivors of the house of Jacob, will no longer rely on him who struck them down but will truly rely on the LORD, the Holy One of Israel.

A remnant will return, a remnant of Jacob will return to the Mighty God. Though your people, O Israel, be like the sand by the sea, only a remnant will return. Destruction has been decreed, overwhelming and righteous. The Lord, the LORD Almighty, will carry out the destruction decreed upon the whole land.

Therefore, this is what the Lord, the LORD Almighty, says: "O my people who live in Zion, do not be afraid of the Assyrians, who beat you with a rod and lift up a club against you, as Egypt did. Very soon my anger against you will end and my wrath will be directed to their destruction." (Isaiah 10:20-25)

5. "Do not listen to Hezekiah. This is what the king of Assyria says: Make peace with me and come out to me. Then every one of you will eat from his own vine and fig tree and drink water from his own cistern, until I come and take you to a land like your own, a land of grain and new wine, a land of bread and vineyards, a land of olive trees and honey. Choose life and not death!

"Do not listen to Hezekiah, for he is misleading you when he says, 'The LORD will deliver us.' " (2 Kings 18:31,32)

In the hope that he had made an impression on many, the terms for surrender are now given. The surrender was to be complete and unconditional. The promise of good treatment was in itself very generous but extremely unlikely in light of Assyrian history, as everyone well knew.

6. "Has the god of any nation delivered his land from the hand of the king of Assyria? Where are the gods of Hamath and Arpad? Where are the gods of Sepharvaim, Hena and Ivvah? Have they rescued Samaria from my hand? Who of all the gods of these countries has been able to save his land from me? How then can the LORD deliver Jerusalem from my hand?" (2 Kings 18:33-35)

In this argument Jehovah was put on the level of the idols. According to the Assyrians, he would be powerless to deliver Jerusalem out of their hands. The time for a decision had come. Assyria gave two options:

1. Surrender to Assyria unconditionally, trusting that the people of Jerusalem would receive good treatment. Or

2. Feel the might of Assyria and be destroyed.

Hezekiah found neither choice acceptable, so he sent a delegation to Isaiah to inform the prophet what the Assyrians had said and how they had spoken against the living God. Even though the people may not have understood the significance of Shear-Jashub, King Hezekiah did. For in the end of his message to Isaiah he said, "Pray for the remnant that still survives." Isaiah responded with words of comfort for Hezekiah:

> "Tell your master, 'This is what the LORD says: Do not be afraid of what you have heard — those words with which the underlings of the king of Assyria have blasphemed me. Listen! I am going to put such a spirit in him that when he hears a certain report, he will return to his own country, and there I will have him cut down with the sword.' "
> (2 Kings 19:6,7)

True to his word, God made Sennacherib hear that Tirhakah, the king of Ethiopia, was coming to attack him with a great army. Believing that he had no time for any kind of siege, he sent back his messengers to try again to get Jerusalem to surrender without a fight or loss of time. This time the argument of surrender was simple and directed to Hezekiah. The king was told that he should not let his God deceive him by promises of deliverance from Assyria. Hezekiah responded with one of the most beautiful prayers ever spoken:

> Hezekiah received the letter from the messengers and read it. Then he went up to the temple of the LORD and spread it out before the LORD. And Hezekiah prayed to the LORD: "O LORD, God of Israel, enthroned between the cherubim,

you alone are God over all the kingdoms of the earth. You have made heaven and earth. Give ear, O LORD, and hear; open your eyes, O LORD, and see; listen to the words Sennacherib has sent to insult the living God.

"It is true, O LORD, that the Assyrian kings have laid waste these nations and their lands. They have thrown their gods into the fire and destroyed them, for they were not gods but only wood and stone, fashioned by men's hands. Now, O LORD our God, deliver us from his hand, so that all kingdoms on earth may know that you alone, O LORD, are God." (2 Kings 19:14-19)

Hezekiah had put it all in the hands of the Lord, asking that he would defend his holy name and deliver them. God's answer in return was also beautiful.

Therefore this is what the LORD says concerning the king of Assyria:

"He will not enter this city or shoot an arrow here. He will not come before it with shield or build a siege ramp against it. By the way that he came he will return; he will not enter this city, declares the LORD. I will defend this city and save it, for my sake and for the sake of David my servant." (2 Kings 19:32-34)

Without any loss to his own army Sennacherib could have left Jerusalem alone. Instead, he had slandered and blasphemed Jehovah. In divine retribution God now sent the mighty Angel of the Lord (the preincarnate Christ) who killed 185,000 of Sennacherib's men that night. It is striking that when Sennacherib speaks of Hezekiah and his campaign against Jerusalem, the best claim he can make is that he shut Hezekiah up in Jerusalem like a bird in a cage. He says nothing about having taken Jerusalem. Indirectly, this is an admission of a defeat; otherwise he surely would have elaborated on his victory.

Any army that loses 185,000 men at one shot has definitely been weakened. Shuzubu the Chaldean, Merodach-

Baladan and Kudur-Nahundu king of Elam saw an opportunity to rebel against Sennacherib. In his fourth campaign Sennacherib marched his troops against the city of Bit Iakin. Very little is recorded of this battle except that Sennacherib was victorious and he established his eldest son Assur nadin shum over the wide land of Sumer and Akkad on Merodach-Baladan's throne. As for Merodach-Baladan and Shuzubu, they escaped into the swamp.

Assur nadin shum had not heard the last of Shuzubu. Under his leadership the rebels, who had escaped from Sennacherib's forces, regrouped and strengthened themselves. With the help of Kurdur-Nahundu, the king of Elam, Shuzubu took over the rule of Sumer and Akkad. It was obvious that Sennacherib was badly needed to put down the rebellion. In his sixth campaign Sennacherib restored Assyrian control. The rebels of Bit Iakin and Elam were deported while their cities were burned and destroyed. On his return march Sennacherib claims to have thrown Shuzubu into bonds of iron and taken him to Assyria.

This is either another exaggeration or somehow Shuzubu must have escaped death, for he returned to the area of Akkad and Sumer. Again he demonstrated his rebellious nature by forming an alliance with Elam and numerous other cities to restore to himself the rule of Sumer and Akkad. The king of Elam who supported Shuzubu this time was Unman Menanu, the younger brother of the deceased Kudur-Nahundu. The revolt was successful and Babylon received Shuzubu as its king about 692.

In order to stop the rebellion once and for all Sennacherib in his eighth campaign attacked this powerful alliance. The number of troops opposing Sennacherib was staggering. He describes their appearance as swarms of locust and the dust raised by their feet as clouds covering the wide heavens. The scene of the battle was the city of Halule on the bank of the Tigris River. The battle was so vicious and Sennacherib so barbarously cruel that some of the details will deliberately be left out. As the battle raged on, Sennacherib boasts how he cut his enemies throats as lambs and made their guts and intestines run down upon the ground. He cut off his enemies' hands to obtain the gold and silver bracelets they wore. The bodies of the dead filled the plain. With his horses prancing victoriously, Sennacherib plunged through the streams of blood, overpowering and slaying his enemies. Babylon felt the full wrath of Sennacherib and was destroyed. Assyria was quick to point out that all this happened because the Babylonians had angered the god Marduk by their rebellions and treaties with Elam. The punishment of Babylon supposedly decreed by the god Marduk was to last for seventy years. During this time the city was not to be rebuilt.

Assyria itself, however, was heading for some unstable times. Apparently Assur nadin shum, Sennacherib's eldest son and the crown prince, had died. Who was to take his place? Sennacherib had three other sons — Adrammelich, Sharezer and Esarhaddon. Normally, the next oldest son would be the obvious choice, but for some reason Sennacherib did not want this to happen. Perhaps there had been some family involvement in Assur nadin shum's death. Be that as it may, Esarhaddon, the youngest, was chosen as Sennacherib's successor and was appointed as the king of Sumer and Akkad. He was also given a new name, Assur etil mukin apla. In a plot to prevent Esarhaddon's succession, Adrammelich and Sharezer fulfilled God's judgment against Sennacherib, for they killed him with the sword. In this way what God had told Hezekiah would happen to Sennacherib for his blasphemy was carried out by his own children.

54

> One day, while he was worshiping in the temple of his god
> Nisroch, his sons Adrammelech and Sharezer cut him down
> with the sword, and they escaped to the land of Ararat. And
> Esarhaddon his son succeeded him as king. (2 Kings 19:37)

They also incited a rebellion against Esarhaddon. Esarhaddon was the wrong one to try this against. His emotions and anger got the best of him and without caution Esarhaddon pursued his brothers.

> To the care of the horses and harnessing of the teams [I
> gave no attention]. My battle equipment I did not gather.
> Provisions for my journey I did not provide. The snow and
> cold of the month of Shabatu, bitter cold, I did not fear. Like
> a swooping bird of prey I opened my hands to bring low my
> foes. I made my way toward Nineveh painfully but quickly.
> Before me, in the land of Hanigalbat, all of their mighty
> warriors blocked my path, offering battle. The terror of the
> great gods, my lords, overwhelmed them. . . . [Some] of their
> number spoke up, "This is our king." . . . As for those villains
> who instigated revolt and rebellion, when they heard of the
> approach of my army, they abandoned their regular troops,
> and fled to parts unknown.[15]

With the defeat and flight of his brothers, Esarhaddon became the undisputed king of Assyria. In the first year of his reign he showed a soft spot in his heart for Babylon. The city had been destroyed by his father Sennacherib and sentenced by the god Marduk to lie in ruins for seventy years. Now in his first year, Esarhaddon devised a plan to rebuild Babylon without going against his father's established foreign policy or the decree of Marduk. His plan was simple. Through soothsayers and oracles it was learned that Marduk, being moved with pity, had turned the record book upside down. The significance of the action is understood when it is noted that the Babylonian numeral seventy upside down is eleven. What a marvelous coincidence it was that his first year as king of Assyria was also the eleventh year Babylon had lain in ruins!

> Seventy years as the period of its desolation he wrote [down in the Book of Fate]. But the merciful Marduk — his anger lasted but a moment — turned [the Book of Fate] upside down and ordered its [the city's] restoration in the eleventh year.[16]

In response to this mercy of Marduk, he sent artists and builders to restore Babylon. He also demonstrated his mercy as well as his submission to Marduk's will by returning to Babylon those who had been deported, along with the possessions which had been plundered. These actions which seem strange for an Assyrian king were most necessary. As we saw, Isaiah declared that God was going to use Babylon to carry his people and their possessions into captivity. This would mean that Babylon would have to rebel and defeat Assyria. That rebellion which would lead to Babylon's dominance was just over fifty years away. It was not the god Marduk who moved Esarhaddon to have Babylon rebuilt. It was the Lord. He had proposed the future and he would bring it to pass.

All seemed to be going smoothly for Assyria until Nabu zer kitti lishir, one of Merodach-Baladan's sons, attacked the city of Ur. In response Esarhaddon marched his army down to the sea-land. In fear Nabu zu kitti lishir fled to Elam, but instead of giving him sanctuary the Elamites killed him with the sword.

Another son of Merodach-Baladan, Na id-Mardu, apparently had fled with his brother to Elam. But when he saw there was no sanctuary in Elam he fled to Esarhaddon and submitted himself, begging mercy. Mercy was granted. Not only was his life spared, but he was also made the king of the entire sea-land area which his brother had ruled before he died. In gratitude he remained a faithful servant of the Assyrian empire.

Some time in the first few years of Esarhaddon's reign Abidi-milkutti, king of Sidon, supported Sanduarri, king of Kundi and Sizu, in a revolt against Assyria. Esarhaddon gathered his men and fought against them. After this victory he demonstrated publicly that he was a true Assyrian. He cut off the kings' heads and hung them on the shoulders of their nobles. Then with singing and music he forced them to parade through Nineveh. The record of colonization that follows is interesting when compared with Ezra. Note that Syria is described as "the Hittite-land" and that it refers to the Philistines.

> I gathered together the kings of the Hittite-land [i.e., Syria] and of the seacoast, all of them. I built a city in another place and called its name Kar-Assur-ah iddina [Esarhaddonburg]. Conquered people [lit., peoples, the conquest of my bow] from the mountains and the sea of the east [rising sun] I settled therein. My official I set over them as governor.[17]

> . . . they came to Zerubbabel and to the heads of the families and said, "Let us help you build because, like you, we seek your God and have been sacrificing to him since the time of Esarhaddon king of Assyria, who brought us here." (Ezra 4:2)

Esarhaddon is clearly credited with the colonization of Samaria, but when did it take place and with what people was it colonized? The most probable answer is that this took place shortly after the defeat of Sidon in the first half of Esarhaddon's reign.

With his domain now under control, Esarhaddon decided to tear down the old palace of Nineveh and build a new one. For the needed supplies and workmen the various kings under his yoke were summoned to come to Nineveh where they received their orders. One of the kings who made this trip to Nineveh was Manasseh, king of Judah.

In the later half of his reign Balu, king of Tyre revolted against Esarhaddon with the help of his friend Tirhakah, king of Ethiopia. In his tenth campaign Esarhaddon defeated Tyre and continued the attack on Tirhakah after a fifteen-day march.

Esarhaddon was victorious and Memphis the royal city of Ethiopia fell to him.

After this tremendous victory Esarhaddon openly displayed his choice of Ashurbanipal, his eldest son, as his successor for the throne of Assyria. He did this by having an image of himself with Ashurbanipal next to him carved in the temple of Assur that was being built. To firmly establish Ashurbanipal in this position Esarhaddon made everyone from the Mediterranean Sea to the Persian Gulf swear that they would accept him as the future king of Assyria. In a further attempt to prevent any future internal problems, Esarhaddon placed Shamash shum ukin, Ashurbanipal's brother, on the throne of Babylon. As a display of generosity and goodwill, Ashurbanipal gave Shamash shum ukin a larger army than Esarhaddon had commanded. Later in his reign Ashurbanipal would deeply regret this kindness shown to his brother.

5. THE FALL OF ASSYRIA AND JUDAH

669-586 B.C.

In 669 Esarhaddon died and Ashurbanipal became the king of Assyria. Tirhakah, king of Ethiopia, tried to take advantage of Esarhaddon's death by revolting against Ashurbanipal. In this revolt Tirhakah retook control of Egypt. The kings and governors that Esarhaddon had established were unable to stand against Tirhakah's army. In desperation a messenger was sent to Nineveh to get help from Ashurbanipal.

When Ashurbanipal heard what Tirhakah was doing, he quickly mobilized the Assyrian army. Tirhakah wisely sent out his army to fight Ashurbanipal's forces while Tirhakah himself remained in Memphis. The battle took place on the open plains, with the Assyrians totally victorious. Realizing that he had no time to lose, Tirhakah fled from Memphis to the city of Thebes in the hope of escaping certain death. As a result the Assyrians attacked and defeated Thebes. Tirhakah escaped but his revolt was smashed. The kings and governors whom he had defeated were reestablished. The most important of them was Necho I, king of Memphis.

As soon, as Ashurbanipal returned to Nineveh, trouble started brewing in the reclaimed territory of Egypt. Now the kings that Ashurbanipal had reestablished started plotting with Tirhakah against Assyria! The plot was discovered by the officials of the army Ashurbanipal had stationed there to

Fall of Jerusalem (2 Kings 25:8-12)

maintain peace and control. He severely punished those who were involved in the plot. Their corpses were hung on stakes and their skin was stripped off and used to cover the city walls. The kings were brought alive to Nineveh to face the wrath of Ashurbanipal personally. Only one king came away with his life and that was Necho. He was returned again to Memphis as its king in great honor.

Tandamane, the nephew of Tirhakah, then took up where Tirhakah left off. He led a powerful revolt against Assyria. Ashurbanipal engaged him in battle. After a bitter fight Egypt and Ethiopia were subdued. As we would expect, Assyria gloated over its victory. The Lord, however, through the Prophet Nahum used these victories of Assyria over Egypt and Ethiopia as a stepping stone to rebuke the pride of Assyria and foretell its fall.

> Are you better than Thebes, situated on the Nile, with water around her? The river was her defense, the waters her wall. Cush and Egypt were her boundless strength; Put and Libya were among her allies. Yet she was taken captive and went into exile. Her infants were dashed to pieces at the head of every street. Lots were cast for her nobles, and all her great men were put in chains. You too will become drunk; you will go into hiding and seek refuge from the enemy.
>
> All your fortresses are like fig trees with their first ripe fruit; when they are shaken, the figs fall into the mouth of the eater. (Nahum 3:8-12)

It was probably at this time and during Ashurbanipal's next three campaigns that the cracks in Assyria's power began to appear. Shamash shum ukin, the king's own brother, who ruled as king of Babylon, was plotting to overthrow him. The biblical account becomes quite interesting in view of this:

> The LORD spoke to Manasseh and his people, but they paid no attention. So the LORD brought against them the

61

> army commanders of the king of Assyria, who took Manasseh prisoner, put a hook in his nose, bound him with bronze shackles and took him to Babylon. (2 Chronicles 33:10,11)

For a long time many have felt that the chronologist made a mistake when he wrote *Babylon* instead of *Nineveh*. The reason it was thought to be a mistake was that Nineveh, not Babylon, was the capital of the king of Assyria. Yet the chronologist does not say that Manasseh was taken to see the king of Assyria. Instead, all he says is that the captain of the army of the king of Assyria carried him to Babylon.

Who was it who imprisoned him in Babylon? It is quite possible that it was Shamash shum ukin, king of Babylon. Many of the captains of the king of Nineveh served and were loyal to Shamash shum ukin above Ashurbanipal, desiring to see him occupy the throne of Assyria instead of Ashurbanipal. This explains three other major problems:

1. Why wasn't Manasseh's arrest and imprisonment recorded in the Assyrian records? It was not recorded because the king of Assyria did not arrest him.

2. What was the purpose of Manasseh's arrest and imprisonment? The purpose was to get him to swear allegiance to Shamash shum ukin instead of Ashurbanipal.

3. Why did Manasseh refortify Judah as is recorded in 2 Chronicles when he returned?

> Afterward he rebuilt the outer wall of the city of David, west of the Gihon spring in the valley, as far as the entrance of the Fish Gate and encircling the hill of Ophel; he also made it much higher. He stationed military commanders in all the fortified cities in Judah. (2 Chronicles 33:14)

He refortified Judah because he knew there was going to be a battle between Ashurbanipal and Shamash shum ukin, a battle in which he wanted no part.

It was not until after Ashurbanipal's fifth or eighth campaign, depending on which cylinder is read, that he found out his brother was plotting against him. In this campaign Elam was defeated and Teumman the king was beheaded. Ashurbanipal established in his place Ummanigash, who had been dethroned by Teumman. On his return march to Nineveh, Ashurbanipal attacked and defeated the people of Gambulu that had aided Elam. These victories and the celebrations afterward were so cruel and vicious that they served as the capstone for Shamash shum ukin's rebellion.

Under him a powerful alliance was formed which might have won if internal problems had not split Elam and starvation had not destroyed Akkad. When there was nothing left to eat, the people turned on Shamash shum ukin and burned him. After this his supporters were seized by Ashurbanipal and killed.

> ... As for those men and their vulgar mouths, who uttered vulgarity against Assur my god, and plotted evil against me, the prince who fears him, I slit their mouths [tongues] and brought them low. The rest of the people, alive by the colossi, between which they had cut down Sennacherib, the father of the father who begot me — at that time, I cut down those people there, as an offering to his shade. Their dismembered bodies I fed to the dogs, swine, wolves and eagles, to the birds of heaven and the fish of the deep.[18]

In place of Shamash shum ukin, Ashurbanipal established Kandalanu as governor of Babylon. Ashurbanipal realized that if he was going to have peace and retain a solid throne, he had to punish all involved in the rebellion. Those who had been involved in the plot also realized what was coming and tried to maintain their rebellion. Because of this Ashurbanipal continued his attacks against Elam. Finally Elam was subdued.

Once the immediate area was defeated, he turned his attention to the other countries that had supported his brother. Those areas included Arabia, Keder and Moab. Uaiti's nephew took over the throne in Arabia but was defeated and transported to Nineveh. In Nineveh he was placed in a kennel with the dogs and as a dog forced to guard the gate of Nineveh. Ammu-ladi, king of Keder, was defeated and given a similar job. He was chained up and forced to watch a kennel. Later Uaiti was also captured and Ashurbanipal put a rope through his jaw and chained him as a dog in a kennel in Nineveh.

It is interesting to note that despite all of the refortifications Manasseh had done Judah was spared. Manasseh had wisely decided not to send aid to Shamash shum ukin. Ashurbanipal therefore had no score to settle with him. Shamash shum ukin was dead and could not take revenge on him for not having helped in the rebellion.

Manasseh died in 644 and was succeeded by Amon, his wicked son. The repentance of Manasseh and his attempts at reform apparently had no affect on Amon. Fortunately he only ruled for two years; in 642 he was assassinated. The nation's response to this violent action is encouraging. The people of the land killed all those who had plotted against the king. Just how much time this took is not known, but it seems most likely that it was not until sometime in 641 that Josiah was made the new king of Judah. The year of 641 was therefore his ascension year, with 640 being his actual first year.

Through all of this Ashurbanipal was still king. The exact date for his death is unknown. The most probable dates given are either 633 and 627. Personally, I think that the date of 633 is most likely correct because when the date of 627 is considered closely as the date for the death of Ashurbanipal, there is a problem. That would mean that Ashuretililani came to the throne in 627. He ruled for four years, which would place his death around 623. At this time he would have been succeeded by his brother Sinsharishkun. Yet already in 626 Nabopolassar was in open rebellion against the Assyrian king, Sinsharishkun. Sinsharishkun therefore had to have become king before 626. In light of this, Ashurbanipal must have died in 633, the seventh year of Josiah king of Judah. The following year ushered in two great changes:

1. Ashuretililani, Ashurbanipal's son, became the new king of Assyria. Incidentally, Kandalanu may have chosen this time to rebel against Assyria.

2. Josiah began to follow the Lord God of Israel.

Very little is known of Ashuretililani except that he re-built the city of Calah. Four years later he died, in 628, and was succeeded by his brother, Sinsharishkun. Under his leadership Assyria went down fast. If any control had been exercised over Judah by Ashuretililani, it ceased with his death. In that year, 626, Nabopolassar rose to power in Babylon. One of his first moves was to make peace with Elam. Under his leadership the Assyrians were driven out of Babylon. Unfortunately, not much is known about the peri-od between 623-616. But after that the history is filled in by the Babylonian Chronicle.

In 616, Nabopolassar's tenth year, the Babylonian army marched up the Euphrates River and defeated the Assyrian army of Sinsharishkun. After plundering several cities, Nabopolassar and his army departed with rich spoils and returned to Babylon. In the meantime, Sinsharishkun en-listed the help of the Egyptians. The Egyptians had thrown off the yoke of Assyria, but saw it to their advantage to oppose the Babylonian-Median alliance. The Egyptian army arrived after Babylon had departed. An attempt was made to overtake them and recover what had been lost. Apparently the Egyptians tired of the pursuit and left. For

65

when the battle finally took place only the defeat of the Assyrian army is mentioned by the Babylonians.

The next year, 615, brought new aggression from Nabopolassar. The city of Ashur was attacked but withstood the assault. The Babylonians withdrew from the city to return to Babylon. This action was viewed as a sign of weakness on Babylon's part and the Assyrian army pursued the Babylonians along the Tigris River as far as the city of Tekrit. There the Babylonian army took its stand. For ten days the Assyrian forces tried in vain to take the city. With their numbers greatly depleted, they returned to Assyria.

The year 614 brought yet more trouble to the once-mighty Assyrian nation. Under Kyaxares, the king of the Medes, Nineveh was attacked and a city in its province was taken. The Medes also attacked the city of Ashur. Nabopolassar mobilized his army to aid the Medes in their assault on Ashur, but he arrived too late. Ashur had already fallen. Because of his intended support a friendship developed between Nabopolassar and Kyaxares.

In 612 Nineveh was again attacked, this time by the combined forces of the Babylonians and Medes. Under their onslaught Nineveh fell. Details of its fall are lacking in the Babylonian Chronicle. The Prophet Nahum, however, sheds some light on how Nineveh fell. When we read his brief account in conjunction with the building inscription of Sennacherib, it forms quite a picture.

> . . . but with an overwhelming flood he will make an end of Nineveh; he will pursue his foes into darkness. (Nahum 1:8)

> The Tebiltu, a raging stream, which from days of old had come up close to the palace, and with its great floods at high water worked havoc with its foundation and destroyed its platform — that small palace I tore down in its totality. The course of the Tebiltu I turned aside from the city's midst, and

directed its outflow into the plain back of the city. Into the water's course I placed four great blocks of limestone and covered them with bitumen; reeds of the cane-brake and rushes I spread over them.

A piece of land, 340 cubits on the side, 289 cubits on the front out of the bed of the Husur (Khosr) River, and the plain about the city, I measured [lit., seized] according to plan. To the plot of the former palace terrace I added it, and raised the whole of it to the height of 190 tipki.

Lest in the passing of days the platform of that terrace should give way before the floods of high water, I built the facing wall round it of great blocks of limestone, and strengthened its structure.[19]

It seems quite probable that this dam was broken down by very high waters or by the invading army when Nineveh fell. If the dam was broken down and the river redirected the area would have no hope. Nineveh would be flooded. Whatever the case, Nineveh fell and became nothing but a mound, a ruined heap.

Ashuruballit, trying to save what was left of the Assyrian Empire, established himself as king in Haran.

In 610, the sixteenth year of Nabopolassar, Babylon and the Medes attacked Haran. The city was taken and plundered. For some reason Ashuruballit was not there. He probably was in Egypt securing help to hold his position. Nabopolassar established a garrison to maintain control of the city of Haran and returned to Babylon.

It was at this time that Josiah king of Judah died, while unsuccessfully trying to prevent this Egyptian army from giving its aid to Ashuruballit. With the aid of the Egyptian army Ashuruballit tried to retake the city of Haran before Nabopolassar could return. His attempt was in vain and now he was out in the open with the Babylonians and the Medes fast approaching. In the battle that followed, the

Medes seemed to have attacked Ashuruballit's forces around the city while Nabopolassar made raids into the hill area of Izalla northeast of Haran.

At this point a step backward in time will help fill in some events in Judah. During these turbulent years a young king, only eight years old, came to the throne of Judah. His name was Josiah. He ruled from 640-609. During his reign he was to produce the greatest reforms in Judah's history. When he was sixteen years old he started to follow the Lord. Four years later, in 628, he took advantage of the crumbling Assyrian Empire and the ascension of the new king Sin-sharishkun and began to purge the land of Judah and Jerusalem. So extensive was his reform that it also reached into the fallen northern land of Israel. A reform of God's people was desperately needed and God would see to it that Josiah would have the time and freedom to do it.

> In the eighth year of his reign, while he was still young, he began to seek the God of his father David. In his twelfth year he began to purge Judah and Jerusalem of high places, Asherah poles, carved idols and cast images. Under his direction the altars of the Baals were torn down; he cut to pieces the incense altars that were above them, and smashed the Asherah poles, the idols and the images. These he broke to pieces and scattered over the graves of those who had sacrificed to them. He burned the bones of the priests on their altars, and so he purged Judah and Jerusalem. In the towns of Manasseh, Ephraim and Simeon, as far as Naphtali, and in the ruins around them, he tore down the altars and the Asherah poles and crushed the idols to powder and cut to pieces all the incense altars thoughout Israel. Then he went back to Jerusalem. (2 Chronicles 34:3-7)

In 622, the eighteenth year of his reign, when Josiah was twenty-six years old, he ordered the temple to be repaired. During the repair work Hilkiah, the high priest, found the

Book of the Law. What a discovery! But why was it found at this time? In order to understand why, it should be noted that it was often the custom to place documents in special places in the foundations of buildings. What better place for the Pentateuch to rest securely than in the foundation of the temple? This foundation was probably cracked in places and in need of repair. It would only be natural that all documents in the foundation be removed during the repairs.

When the Book of the Law which had been found was read by Shaphan to Josiah, Josiah tore his clothes. He realized that he and his nation were under the wrath of God because their fathers had not kept the commandments of God's Law. The Prophetess Huldah confirmed Josiah's worst fears that Judah was under God's judgment for its unfaithfulness. In response, Josiah's reform took hold quickly and firmly among the people. He also had the people observe the Passover and swear that they would return to the Lord God of Israel. How wonderfully God blessed them as they followed the reforms of Josiah!

In the year 609, Josiah's thirty-first year and Nabopolassar's seventeenth year, the history of Judah, Babylon and Assyria came together again. Ashuruballit secured help from Egypt in hope of retaking Haran. While this Egyptian army under Pharaoh Necho was going up through the land of Israel, Josiah attempted to stop him at the pass of Megiddo. In the ensuing battle Josiah was killed. He had been the godliest king since David.

In his place Jehoahaz his son became the next king. He ruled for only three months and then was deposed by Pharaoh Necho, who was on his way back to Egypt. Necho appointed as the next king of Judah Eliakim, another son of Josiah, and changed his name to Jehoiakim. It is difficult even to believe that this wicked, ungodly man could have been Josiah's son.

The year 605 brought great changes. The Babylonian army under Nebuchadnezzar and the Egyptian forces clashed at Carchemish, with the Egyptians suffering a devastating defeat, as the Babylonian records say:

> In the twenty-first year the king of Akkad stayed in his own land. Nebuchadnezzar his eldest son, the crown-prince, mustered [the Babylonian army] and took command of his troops. He marched to Carchemish which is on the bank of the Euphrates, and crossed the river to go against the Egyptian army which lay in Carchemish.
>
> They fought with each other and the Egyptian army withdrew before him. He accomplished their defeat and [beat them] into non-existence. As for the rest of the Egyptian army, which had escaped from the defeat so quickly that no weapon had reached them, in the district of Hamath the Babylonian troops overtook and defeated them so that not a single man escaped to his own country.
>
> At that time Nebuchadnezzar conquered the whole area of the Hatti-country.[20]

Meanwhile in Babylon Nabopolassar died. In haste Nebuchadnezzar marched back with some of his army across the desert to return to Babylon and claim the throne. Once there he became the new king of Babylon. With the throne securely his he returned to the land of Syria and Palestine. It was probably on this return trip that Jehoiakim submitted to Nebuchadnezzar and the first deportation took place, of which Daniel and his three companions were part.

> For twenty-one years Nabopolassar had been king of Babylon. On the eighth of the month of Ab he died [lit., the fates]. In the month of Elul Nebuchadnezzar returned to Babylon and on the first day of the month of Elul he sat on the royal throne in Babylon.
>
> In the "accession year" Nebuchadnezzar went back again to the Hatti-land and until the month of Sebat marched

unopposed through the Hatti-land. In the month of Sebat he
took the heavy tribute of the Hatti-territory to Babylon.
    In the month of Nisan he took the hands of Bel and the son
of Bel and celebrated the Skitu [New Year's] festival.[21]

From 604 through 602 B.C., Jehoiakim was a faithful
vassal of Babylon. But in 601 he saw an opportunity to rebel.
Egypt and Babylon had clashed again in battle and both had
sustained heavy losses.

> In the fourth year the king of Akkad mustered his army
> and marched to the Hatti-land. In the Hatti-land they
> marched unopposed. In the month of Kislev he took the lead
> of his army and marched to Egypt. The king of Egypt heard
> of it and mustered his army. In open battle they smote the
> breast of each other and inflicted great havoc on each other.
> The king of Akkad and his troops turned back and returned
> to Babylon.
> In the fifth year the king of Akkad stayed in his own land
> and gathered together his chariots and horses in great
> numbers.[22]

Seizing the opportunity Jehoiakim rebelled, as did many
other kingdoms. Since Nebuchadnezzar remained in Babylon the following year, there was an immediate power struggle. Judah received the brunt of it on all sides.

> During Jehoiakim's reign, Nebuchadnezzar king of Baby-
> lon invaded the land, and Jehoiakim became his vassal for
> three years. But then he changed his mind and rebelled
> against Nebuchadnezzar. The LORD sent Babylonian [Chal-
> dean], Aramean, Moabite and Ammonite raiders against
> him. He sent them to destroy Judah in accordance with the
> word of the LORD proclaimed by his servants the prophets.
> (2 Kings 24:1,2)

The power struggle took place in Nebuchadnezzar's absence as the Babylonian records show. Since they are called
"raiders," this was not an official army sent out. Nor was it
headed by Nebuchadnezzar.

By 599 Nebuchadnezzar had rebuilt his army and was on the march again to punish those nations who had rebelled against him in his absence. The first to feel his might were the Arabs. The plunder he took included animals and valuable possessions, undoubtedly to strengthen his army. He also took their gods to make them a submissive people. The following year he came against Judah. Three months and ten days before Judah fell, Jehoiakim died.

> Jehoiachin was eighteen years old when he became king, and he reigned in Jerusalem three months and ten days. (2 Chronicles 36:9)

The account in 2 Kings adds to this:

> At that time the officers of Nebuchadnezzar king of Babylon advanced on Jerusalem and laid siege to it. (2 Kings 24:10)

The Babylonian Chronicles add:

> In the seventh year, the month of Kislev, the king of Akkad mustered his troops, marched to the Hatti-land, and encamped against the city of Judah and on the second day of the month of Adar he seized the city and captured the king. He appointed there a king of his own choice [lit., heart], received its heavy tribute and sent them to Babylon. In the eighth year, the month of Tebet, the king of Akkad marched to Hatti-land as far as Carchemish.[23]

Since Judah fell to Nebuchadnezzar on March 16, 597 B.C., the date for Jehoiakim's death would be early December. How he died is not revealed. The only thing known for sure is that he received the burial of an ass as Jeremiah had prophesied.

> Therefore this is what the LORD says about Jehoiakim son of Josiah king of Judah: "They will not mourn for him: 'Alas, my brother! Alas, my sister!' They will not mourn for him: 'Alas, my master! Alas, his splendor!' He will have the

burial of a donkey — dragged away and thrown outside the gates of Jerusalem." (Jeremiah 22:18,19)

Therefore this is what the LORD says about Jehoiakim king of Judah: He will have no one to sit on the throne of David; his body will be thrown out and exposed to the heat by day and the frost by night. (Jeremiah 36:30)

It is also interesting to note that in foretelling Jehoiakim's death Jeremiah had mentioned the heat of the day and frost at night. This would coincide with the time of year given for his death. Jehoiachin was appointed as the next king, but when Judah fell Nebuchadnezzar deposed him and appointed Mattaniah as the new king. He also changed his name from Mattaniah to Zedekiah (Jehovah is righteous). It seems strange that such a name which glorified the God of Israel should be given by Nebuchadnezzar unless it is remembered that by this time Daniel had the position in Babylon as chief interpreter of dreams.

In Nebuchadnezzar's tenth year (595 B.C.), internal problems touched off a revolt that threatened to rip Babylon apart.

In the tenth year the king of Akkad was in his own land; from the month of Kislev to the month of Tebet, there was rebellion in Akkad. . . . With arms he slew many of his own army. His own hand captured his enemy. . . . He marched to the Hatti-land, where kings and officials came before him and he received their heavy tribute and then returned [to Babylon].[24]

It is not known for sure who led this revolt against Nebuchadnezzar. It is possible, as some have concluded, that the leader of the rebellion was Baba-ahu-iddina, the son of Nabu-ahhe-bullit. Nabu-ahhe-bullit had been rewarded and promoted by Nebuchadnezzar's father himself. Though a prominent man, Baba-ahu-iddina was tried and convicted for breaking the royal oath and causing insurrection. His property was confiscated and he was executed. His death took place in the eleventh year of Nebuchadnezzar.

Because of the recent rebellion Nebuchadnezzar now had to go about strengthening the kingdom in his own land. That also meant taking oaths of loyalty. The eleventh year of Nebuchadnezzar brought Judah back into the picture. Zedekiah was summoned to Babylon, most likely to promise that he would remain a faithful vassal of Nebuchadnezzar. Jeremiah gives the date:

> This is the message Jeremiah gave to the staff officer Seraiah son of Neriah, the son of Mahseiah, when he went to Babylon with Zedekiah king of Judah in the fourth year of his reign. (Jeremiah 51:59)

Unfortunately, Zedekiah and Jerusalem did not live up to their oath of loyalty. Instead, they continuously flirted with Egypt. Finally, in 588 in the ninth year of Zedekiah, the tenth month, Babylon came against Jerusalem to destroy it once and for all. In the first part of the siege Jeremiah succeeded in getting the inhabitants of Jerusalem to obey what the Lord had required of them, that they set free their Hebrew bondmen and not keep them in continuous bondage. But when the Babylonians temporarily withdrew from Jerusalem because of the Egyptian army, they hardened their hearts and broke the oath of freedom that they had made in the name of the Lord. In just recompense God had this to say to them through the Prophet Jeremiah:

> The word came to Jeremiah from the LORD after King Zedekiah had made a covenant with all the people in Jerusalem to proclaim freedom for the slaves. Everyone was to free his Hebrew slaves, both male and female; no one was to hold a fellow Jew in bondage. So all the officials and people who entered into this covenant agreed that they would free their

male and female slaves and no longer hold them in bondage. They agreed, and set them free. But afterward they changed their minds and took back the slaves they had freed and enslaved them again.

Then the word of the LORD came to Jeremiah: "This is what the LORD, the God of Israel, says: I made a covenant with your forefathers when I brought them out of Egypt, out of the land of slavery. I said, 'Every seventh year each of you must free any fellow Hebrew who has sold himself to you. After he has served you six years, you must let him go free.' Your fathers, however, did not listen to me or pay attention to me. Recently you repented and did what is right in my sight: Each of you proclaimed freedom to his countrymen. You even made a covenant before me in the house that bears my Name. But now you have turned around and profaned my name: each of you has taken back the male and female slaves you had set free to go where they wished. You have forced them to become your slaves again.

"Therefore, this is what the LORD says: You have not obeyed me; you have not proclaimed freedom for your fellow countrymen. So I now proclaim 'freedom' for you, declares the LORD — 'freedom' to fall by the sword, plague and famine. I will make you abhorrent to all the kingdoms of the earth. The men who have violated my covenant and have not fulfilled the terms of the covenant they made before me, I will treat like the calf they cut in two and then walked between its pieces. The leaders of Judah and Jerusalem, the court officials, the priests and all the people of the land who walked between the pieces of the calf, I will hand over to their enemies who seek their lives. Their dead bodies will become food for the birds of the air and the beasts of the earth.

"I will hand Zedekiah king of Judah and his officials over to their enemies who seek their lives, to the army of the king of Babylon, which has withdrawn from you. I am going to give the order, declares the LORD, and I will bring them back to this city. They will fight against it, take it and burn it down. And I will lay waste the towns of Judah so no one can live there." (Jeremiah 34:8-22)

In 586, the eleventh year of Zedekiah, the fourth month, Jerusalem fell. In an attempt to save themselves, Zedekiah, his sons and the Jewish leaders tried to flee toward Jericho but they were captured and taken to Nebuchadnezzar. Zedekiah was then made to watch as the Babylonians killed his sons before his eyes. Then, so that the memory would never leave him and so that he could never see anything beautiful after that sight, he was blinded. After that he was taken to Babylon. In these actions what seemed like a contradiction between Jeremiah and Ezekiel was fulfilled in perfect harmony. Jeremiah had said that Zedekiah would see Nebuchadnezzar face to face and be taken to Babylon; Ezekiel had prophesied that Zedekiah would never see Babylon.

As for Jerusalem — it was destroyed and plundered. The time of God's people having their own king was over. Never again would they have a king until the true King of kings would come to them.

6. HARMONY IS POSSIBLE
841-700 B.C.

Throughout the years the Bible has suffered greatly at the hands of man. Every time man comes across something that doesn't seem to make sense to him, he says that the Bible must be wrong because he feels he is right.

One of the areas that has been attacked most consistently is the chronology of the kings in the Old Testament. That period of history, as we have it in the Bible, is said to be irreconcilable and the clearest example that the Bible cannot be inspired by God because it obviously contains errors.

In *The Mysterious Numbers of the Hebrew Kings* Edwin Thiele makes use of the numbers of the kings as written in Scripture and tries to explain how they fit together. Although he has done this successfully in the kingdom of Judah until the time of Joash and in the Northern Kingdom until the time of Jehu, in the following period of time until Hezekiah and Hoshea some of his conclusions contradict the inspiration of Scripture. The Bible's chronology is treated as something that evolved through time. The following quotes illustrate Thiele's views:

> It is extremely unlikely that official court recorders would set down such iniquitous deeds of rulers as are found in the biblical records. Nor is it likely that nations so often at war with each other would date the accessions of their rulers according to the years of enemy kings. . . . Such recordings could be expected from the prophetic schools but not from the palace of Israel's kings. And it is extremely

unlikely that the nefarious deeds of Jezebel were set down by one of Ahab's recorders.[25]

Centuries later when the seemingly inadequate documents of this period came into the hands of the final editors of Kings, the exact situation that prevailed in 752 B.C. was not understood and the employment of dual dating for the synchronism of 2 Kings 15:27 for the accession of Pekah was not perceived.[26]

In his discussion of the years 841 to 723 B.C. Thiele states:

> The period before us is one of the most interesting in Hebrew history from a chronological standpoint. The problems here with the biblical data have long defied all efforts of scholars to find the solutions.[27]

What Thiele says is indeed true; this period of time is indeed interesting. The following is a presentation of the chronology of the Hebrew kings in that questionable time. If one considers this puzzle carefully, he can see that all the biblical numbers for the Hebrew kings are correct as we have them. They all fit together chronologically, and if they do not seem to fit together it is only because mankind has not been able to understand them properly.

The key to being able to understand this period of chronology is to go to a time when we are sure of the dates. Such a time and date is the fall of the Northern Kingdom. Thiele in his book *The Mysterious Numbers of the Hebrew Kings* gives the date as 723. In 2 Kings 18:10 we read:

> At the end of three years the Assyrians took it. So Samaria was captured in Hezekiah's sixth year, which was the ninth year of Hoshea king of Israel.

Here it clearly refers to Hezekiah's sixth year. Therefore, we know the date of Hezekiah's sixth year. It was 723. The next Bible passage is 2 Kings 18:9:

> In King Hezekiah's fourth year, which was the seventh year of Hoshea son of Elah king of Israel, Shalmaneser

king of Assyria marched against Samaria and laid siege to it.

The fourth year of Hezekiah, then, was 725 and the seventh year of Hoshea was 725. The next Bible reference is 2 Kings 18:1,2:

> In the third year of Hoshea son of Elah king of Israel, Hezekiah son of Ahaz king of Judah began to reign. He was twenty-five years old when he became king, and he reigned in Jerusalem twenty-nine years.

The third year of Hoshea was 729; the first year of Hezekiah was 729. We know that Hezekiah reigned for 29 years. Therefore, his last year of reign would be 700. However, when Hezekiah's reign is considered as being from 729-700, we have to confront one of the most perplexing problems in the Old Testament.

We know that in 701 Sennacherib came against Judah. This is called the fourteenth year of Hezekiah's reign, but we know that 701 would be in his twenty-eighth year. Yet we also know that Hezekiah's life was extended by fifteen years. Since he reigned for twenty-nine years he would have been sick unto death in his fourteenth year. God then added on fifteen years to equal twenty-nine years; this was his total reign.

Because of the way things were recorded in Isaiah and Kings, people have long felt that the Babylonian visit came right after Sennacherib had invaded the land. Thus, both the invasion and the visit were in the same fourteenth year. This opinion does not seem to be the best understanding of the situation for the following six reasons:

1. One thing beyond question is that in his fourteenth year Hezekiah became sick unto death and God granted him fifteen more years. Hezekiah's sickness then would have taken place in 715. Of this we can be sure. However, when

you look at the date 715 and say that Sennacherib invaded in *that* fourteenth year it does not fit. Sennacherib did not reign until 704. It was his father Sargon, who was reigning from 721-705 in Hezekiah's fourteenth year. Therefore the king who was on the throne of Assyria in 715 was Sargon, not Sennacherib.

2. The second argument against having Sennacherib's campaign in *this* fourteenth year of Hezekiah before he became sick is found in 2 Kings 20:6:

> I will add fifteen years to your life. And I will deliver you and this city from the hand of the king of Assyria. I will defend this city for my sake and for the sake of my servant David.

In this passage God says that he will deliver Hezekiah and Jerusalem out of the hand of the king of Assyria. This promise would not make sense if God had already delivered Judah out of the hand of Assyria. God further said, "I will defend this city for my sake." Again, it would not make sense for God to say this if he had already defended it. The Prophet Isaiah records God's reply to proud Sennacherib; here we see just how God defended Jerusalem for his own sake:

> Who is it you have insulted and blasphemed? Against whom have you raised your voice and lifted your eyes in pride? Against the Holy One of Israel!
> I will defend this city and save it, for my sake and for the sake of David my servant!
> Then the angel of the LORD went out and put to death a hundred and eighty-five thousand men in the Assyrian camp. When the people got up the next morning — there were all the dead bodies! (Isaiah 37:23,35,36)

3. A third argument against the Assyrians under Sennacherib invading in *this* fourteenth year of Hezekiah is found in 2 Kings 18:15,16:

> So Hezekiah gave him all the silver that was found in the
> temple of the LORD and in the treasuries of the royal palace.
> At this time Hezekiah king of Judah stripped off the gold
> with which he had covered the doors and doorposts of the
> temple of the LORD, and gave it to the king of Assyria.

Note the extent to which Hezekiah had to go to pay off
Sennacherib. Comparing this verse to 2 Kings 20:13 we find
that when Hezekiah received the Babylonian messengers,
Hezekiah's wealth was not in a stripped condition.

> Hezekiah received the messengers and showed them all
> that was in his storehouses — the silver, the gold, the spices
> and the fine oil — his armory and everything found among
> his treasures. There was nothing in his palace or in all his
> kingdom that Hezekiah did not show them.

It would be almost impossible, in the same year he had
stripped everything and given it to the Assyrians, for Hezekiah to be able to impress the Babylonian messengers with
all his riches.

4. The fourth argument is: Even if Sennacherib invaded
in the beginning of the year 715, it is very difficult to try to
squeeze all the events that took place into one year. Sennacherib would have to come up against Judah two times,
send messengers to talk to Jerusalem and have the messengers return back to him with a reply; his army would have
to be defeated; news of it would have to travel 600 miles to
Babylon; and the Babylonians would have to send their
messengers 600 miles to Judah. The enormity of all this
seems almost impossible to fit into one year's time.

5. The fifth argument raises a question. Does the Bible
list the visit of the Babylonians before or after the invasion
of Sennacherib? When Kings and Isaiah record the events
that happened in Hezekiah's life *after* Sennacherib is mentioned, they say:

> In those days Hezekiah became ill and was at the point of death. The prophet Isaiah son of Amoz went to him and said, "This is what the LORD says: Put your house in order, because you are going to die; you will not recover." (2 Kings 20:1)

> In those days Hezekiah became ill and was at the point of death. The prophet Isaiah son of Amoz went to him and said, "This is what the LORD says: Put your house in order, because you are going to die; you will not recover." (Isaiah 38:1)

The conclusion people have reached is that after Sennacherib invaded, Hezekiah became sick. But the expression "in those days" does not have to mean that. It is an idiomatic expression and it can mean "in the days of Hezekiah this happened." If this is the meaning, then portions of 2 Chronicles take on added interest:

> In those days Hezekiah became ill and was at the point of death. He prayed to the LORD, who answered him and gave him a miraculous sign. (2 Chronicles 32:24)

It is my opinion that verses 24-30 list the events of Hezekiah in chronological order starting at the day when he was sick in 715. Then he received a sign (verse 25):

> But Hezekiah's heart was proud and he did not respond to the kindness shown him; therefore the LORD's wrath was on him and on Judah and Jerusalem.

How had he failed to respond to the kindness shown him? When the Babylonians came, he did not glorify God and tell them this was a marvelous recovery from God. Therefore he fell under God's wrath. The following verses talk about Hezekiah's tremendous wealth. Then in verse 30 it says:

> It was Hezekiah who blocked the upper outlet of the Gihon spring and channeled the water down to the west side of the City of David.

This event took place later in Hezekiah's reign when Sennacherib came against the city, as 2 Chronicles 32 states:

> When Hezekiah saw that Sennacherib had come and that he intended to make war on Jerusalem, he consulted with his officials and military staff about blocking off the water from the springs outside the city, and they helped him. A large force of men assembled, and they blocked all the springs and the stream that flowed through the land. "Why should the kings of Assyria come and find plenty of water?" they said. (2 Chronicles 32:2-4)

Therefore, in the chronology of events described in 2 Chronicles 32:24-30, the Babylonians paid their visit before the Assyrian forces of Sennacherib besieged the city of Jerusalem. What then do we do with the fourteenth year of Hezekiah when Sennacherib invaded? If it was not in 715, when was it? There really is a very easy and logical explanation.

As Thiele has pointed out, the Jews dated from many events. The following two examples demonstrate that they dated so many years from the Exodus or from the split into the Northern and Southern Kingdoms.

> In the four hundred and eightieth year after the Israelites had come out of Egypt, in the fourth year of Solomon's reign over Israel, in the month of Ziv, the second month, he began to build the temple of the LORD. (1 Kings 6:1)

> There was no more war until the thirty-fifth year of Asa's reign. (2 Chronicles 15:19)

This example from 2 Chronicles is especially interesting, because the thirty-fifth year of Asa was really his fifteenth year. The reason for saying the thirty-fifth year was that thirty-five years had passed since the schism between Israel and Judah.

With this in mind it becomes extremely fascinating when you isolate the first fourteen years of Hezekiah's life from the following fifteen. Those later fifteen years were a new God-given lease on life and very rightly set aside. In view of that, the fourteenth year after Hezekiah's recovery in 715 would be 701. What events happened in 701? We know them very well, for this is when Sennacherib invaded Judah as 2 Kings 18:13 records:

> In the fourteenth year of King Hezekiah's reign, Sennacherib king of Assyria attacked all the fortified cities of Judah and captured them.

It may be very difficult to change our minds from thinking of Sennacherib invading prior to the visit of the Babylonians and putting him fourteen years later. But dating the Assyrian invasion from Hezekiah's recovery does answer an apparent chronological problem in the Bible. Most important though, instead of changing the numbers or disagreeing with what God has said, it allows the Bible to stand as it is. There are many arguments in support of putting the Babylonians before the Assyrian invasion, but no really convincing arguments for putting it after.

6. The final argument (and the one I feel is the most powerful) is that when the Babylonians are put in 715 and the Assyrians in 701 all the rest of the numbers of the Hebrew kings fall right in line. What greater testimony could there be?

The following pages will now build on this 715 B.C. dating. There are two ways of figuring out the dates for events. One way is to go forward in time, the other is to go backward in time. For this period of history figuring backward in time is easier. The time period that will be covered is from 715 in Judah to the first year of Joash in 835. In Israel the time period that will be covered is from the fall of Israel in 723 to the first year of Jehu in 841.

Once more we need to consider the date of Hezekiah's first year, 729. The passage to take into account is 2 Kings 17:1.

> In the twelfth year of Ahaz king of Judah, Hoshea son of Elah became king of Israel in Samaria, and he reigned nine years.

If, as we have seen, Hoshea's seventh year was 725 and his third year was 729, Hoshea's first year had to be 732. Ahaz's twelfth year then also had to be 732, making his first year 744 and his last year 728. Moreover, Pekah, the king in Israel prior to Hoshea, ruled for twenty years; he reigned from 752 to 732. In 2 Kings 16:1 we are told:

> In the seventeenth year of Pekah son of Remaliah, Ahaz son of Jotham began to reign.

The seventeenth year would be 735. At first glance this seems to cause a problem with the dating of Ahaz; for if Ahaz's twelfth year was 732, and his first year was 744, how can the writer in 2 Kings say that Ahaz began to rule in the seventeenth year of Pekah, namely 735? As we will see later, this is a reference to his first year of sole reign in 735, not the beginning of his reign in 744.

In 2 Kings 15:32 we read:

> In the second year of Pekah son of Remaliah king of Israel, Jotham son of Uzziah king of Judah began to reign.

Pekah, as we noticed, had his seventeenth year in 735. Pekah's second year, then, would have been 750. Jotham it would seem — again only at first glance — came to the throne in 750.

A problem immediately arises when that verse is compared with 2 Kings 15:30, where it says that Hoshea made a plot against Pekah, and he struck him and killed him in the twentieth year of Jotham. Pekah, as we noted, died in 732. The twentieth year of Jotham would therefore have to be 732, making his reign begin in 752. But how can Jotham's first year in 752 be the same as Pekah's second year in 750? Again, it seems as if we have a contradiction.

How this can be is easily explained. Uzziah, in the year 752, had reigned for thirty-nine years. He would have been fifty-five or fifty-six years old. It would be time for his son to start his training as the next king. As we have also seen, the rapid decentralization and struggle for power in the Northern Kingdom after Jeroboam II died may have made this move seem wise. This would result in a coregency beginning in 753. In 750 Uzziah tried to usurp the priest's role and was turned into a leper. This would require Jotham to assume full rule in 750 and could properly be called his first year — that is, his first sole year.

Another question arises in comparing the verses; 2 Kings 15:32 says that Jotham reigned sixteen years and 2 Kings 15:30 refers to his twentieth year. The problem causes no great difficulty. Perhaps he was an invalid or very sick and not able to carry out his reign, and so he had passed on the throne to his son; or Ahaz may have taken it from him, but they still dated it according to Jotham's reign because he was alive even though he reigned only sixteen years. It becomes even more interesting when you remember that in the seventeenth year of Pekah, Ahaz began to rule. The seventeenth year of Jotham would have been 735 but the throne was not his for, as we saw in 2 Kings 16:1, Ahaz began to reign in that

year. The seventeenth year of Pekah, then, was Ahaz's first
sole year of reign, having stripped the throne from his father
Jotham. In 2 Kings 15:27 we read:

> In the fifty-second year of Azariah king of Judah, Pekah
> son of Remaliah became king of Israel in Samaria, and he
> reigned twenty years.

Was the fifty-second year of Uzziah's reign Pekah's first
year in 752? A comparison of 2 Kings 15 verses 17,13,14,8
and 1 shows that this is not possible. As others have correct-
ly noted, this is a period that has dual dating. Pekah's reign
dated back along with the beginning of Menahem's in 752
because of the position of power he held east of the Jordan.
What about the fifty-second year of Uzziah, then? In 2 Kings
15:13,17 we read:

> Shallum son of Jabesh became king in the thirty-ninth
> year of Uzziah king of Judah, and he reigned in Samaria
> one month.

> In the thirty-ninth year of Azariah king of Judah, Mena-
> hem son of Gadi became king of Israel, and he reigned in
> Samaria ten years.

Menahem reigned for ten years, from 752 to 742, with
Pekah in a ruling position on the east side of the Jordan.
This also established 752 as Uzziah's thirty-ninth year,
agreeing with Jotham's date in his first year of coregency in
752. Then in 741 his son Pekahiah, as we learn from 2 Kings
15:23, ruled for two years (741-740).

> In the fiftieth year of Azariah king of Judah, Pekahiah son
> of Menahem became king of Israel in Samaria, and he
> reigned two years.

Uzziah's fiftieth year was in 741, therefore Pekahiah began to rule in 742. In his second year (740) Pekahiah was
killed by Pekah. This clearly establishes the date for Pekah's

first sole year and also the fifty-second year of Uzziah, as was previously indicated by 2 Kings 15:27.

> In the fifty-second year of Azariah king of Judah, Pekah son of Remaliah became king of Israel in Samaria, and he reigned twenty years.

Next we go to Zechariah and Shallum. Zechariah ruled for six months in the thirty-eighth year of Uzziah's reign which would put him at 753, and Shallum ruled for one month in 753, according to 2 Kings 15:8,13:

> In the thirty-eighth year of Azariah king of Judah, Zechariah son of Jeroboam became king of Israel in Samaria and he reigned six months.

> Shallum son of Jabesh became king in the thirty-ninth year of Uzziah king of Judah, and he reigned in Samaria one month.

All that is needed to find out the next step in the history of the kings is to go to 2 Kings 15:1:

> In the twenty-seventh year of Jeroboam king of Israel, Azariah son of Amaziah king of Judah began to reign.

Here it mentions that in the twenty-seventh year of Jeroboam, Uzziah began to reign. To figure out the twenty-seventh year of Jeroboam we need to subtract twenty-seven from forty-one because Jeroboam reigned forty-one years. Then we need to add fourteen years to the year before Zechariah, 754. That brings us to the date of 768 as Jeroboam's twenty-seventh year and makes his first year in 795.

In 2 Kings 15:1 we read that the twenty-seventh year of Jeroboam, 768, was Uzziah's first year and yet we know that 753 was Uzziah's thirty-eighth year. The only thing it can possibly mean when referring to that as his *first* year is, that it was his *first sole year*. Amaziah, his father, would then have died in the year 768. Amaziah ruled for twenty-nine years. Therefore, Amaziah's first year would be 797.

With that information, 2 Kings 14:23 becomes interesting when it says:

> In the fifteenth year of Amaziah son of Joash king of Judah, Jeroboam son of Jehoash king of Israel became king in Samaria, and he reigned forty-one years.

This says that the fifteenth year of Amaziah was Jeroboam's first year, his first sole year, 782. If you take Amaziah's reign of twenty-nine years and make 782 his fifteenth year, he would live for fourteen more years and die in 768; that was Uzziah's first sole year.

2 Kings 14:17 is important, for it says Amaziah lived after the death of Jehoash fifteen years.

> Amaziah son of Joash king of Judah lived for fifteen years after the death of Jehoash son of Jehoahaz king of Israel.

Now if Amaziah died in 768, that means Jehoash died around 782. This would confirm the 782 dating of Jeroboam's first full year of reign, which was Amaziah's fifteenth year. Knowing Jehoash's last year of reign, we need to add sixteen years to find out when he began his reign. Sixteen years would bring us to 798 at which time, according to 2 Kings 13:10, Joash of Judah was in his thirty-seventh year.

> In the thirty-seventh year of Joash king of Judah, Jehoash son of Jehoahaz became king of Israel in Samaria, and he reigned sixteen years.

This would mean that the date for Joash's reign was 798 in his thirty-seventh year. In the twenty-third year of Joash of Judah, 812, Jehoahaz began to reign in Israel. 2 Kings 12:1 says:

> In the seventh year of Jehu, Joash became king, and he reigned in Jerusalem forty years.

In 2 Kings 12:1 we learn that the seventh year of Jehu, Joash began to reign. Joash began to reign in 835 when

Athaliah was killed. Jehu's seventh year then was 835. His first year would have been 841. Jehu reigned for twenty-eight years. This confirms the date of 812 for Jehoahaz's first year.

We have now covered what many Bible scholars consider the most difficult chronological period. Yet the harmony of Scripture has not been attacked or broken. That is how it should be. It always has been true and always will be true that when man thinks he has found a mistake in the Holy Scriptures, he can be sure of one thing — he is mistaken, not the Scriptures. God's Word remains unshaken.

Judah   Timeline   Israel
841-586 B.C.

Judah			Israel
	840	841	Jehu's 1st year
Joash's 1st year	835	835	Jehu's 7th year
	820		
		813	Jehu's death
Joash's 23rd year	812	812	Jehoahaz's 1st year
	800		

	800		
Joash's 37th year	798	798	Jehoash's 1st year
Amaziah's 1st year	797		
	795		
		783	Jehoash died in 783 or beginning of 782 Completed 15 years
Amaziah's 15th year	782	782	Jeroboam's 1st sole year
	780		
Amaziah's 29th & last year Uzziah's 1st sole year	768	768	Jeroboam's 27th year
	760		
		754	Jeroboam's 41st & last year
Uzziah's 38th year	753	753	Zechariah's 6 month rule
Uzziah's 39th year + Jotham's 1st year	752	752	Pekah's 1st year & Menahem's 1st year
Jotham's 1st sole year	750	750	Pekah's 2nd year
Ahaz's 1st year	744		
		742	Menahem's 10th & last year
Uzziah's 50th year +	741	741	Pekahiah's 1st year
	740		Pekahiah's 2nd & last year
Uzziah's 52nd year	739	739	Pekah's 1st sole year
Jotham's 16th year	736		
Ahaz's 1st sole year	735	735	Pekah's 17th year
Jotham's 20th year, Ahaz's 12th year	732	732	Hoshea's 1st year
Hezekiah's 1st year	729	729	Hoshea's 3rd year
Ahaz's 16th & last year	728		
Hezekiah's 4th year	725	725	Hoshea's 7th year
Hezekiah's 6th year	723	723	Fall of Northern Kingdom
	720		

91

	720
Hezekiah's 14th year	715
Sennacherib's invasion	701
Hezekiah's 29th & last year	700

Manasseh	699-644	55 years
Amon	643-642	2 years
Rebellion & Josiah ascension	641	
Josiah	640-609	31 years
Jehoahaz	609	3 months
Jehoiakim	609-598	11 years
Jehoiachin	598	3 months
Zedekiah	597-586	11 years

7. DICTIONARY OF KINGS
931-586 B.C.

ASSYRIA

Tukulti-Urta II	890-884	Took vigorous action against the desert and Aramean tribes. Assyria on the rise.
Ashurnasirpal II	883-859	Extremely cruel. Conquered the tribes of the middle Euphrates, extended Assyrian control over to the Upper Sea. Kept clear of Damascus and Israel. In his building project to enlarge Calah he used over 50,000 prisoners. Also began work on the Zigurat.
Shalmaneser III	858-824	In 857 he captured Carchemish. Fought against Syria, Israel and nine other cities at Karkar in 853. Ahab supplied 2,000 chariots and 10,000 footmen; Ben-Hadad supplied 1,000 chariots and 20,000 footmen; Irhuleni supplied 700 chariots. In 849, 848 and 845 Shalmaneser again attacked Ben-Hadad. After the death of Ben-Hadad he attacked Hazael. Jehu not only left Hazael to fight alone, but also sent tribute to Assyria. His son Assurdaninapli led a revolt against him which enabled Hazael to grow in strength.

ASSYRIA

Shamsiadad V	823-810	Had to reunite Assyria because of the rebellion Assurdaninapli had caused. Led three campaigns against Babylon and Fort Der. When he died young, his wife, Semiramis, took control of the throne and held it until his son, Adadnirari III, was old enough to take over, giving her a reign of five years, from 810-805.
Adadnirari III	805-783	A powerful king. Seems to have defeated Hazael twice between the years of 805-803. He was most likely the answer God gave to Jehoahaz's prayer for help. Claims to have returned Israel to the position of his tributary. In the last half of his reign Assyria began to decline in power.
Shalmaneser IV	782-773	Was unable to stop the deterioration of Assyria, which had started in the latter half of Adadnirari's reign. In 773 he died young and childless. It is possible that at this time Jonah came to Assyria.
Ashurdan III	772-775	Unable to reverse the problems in Assyria. In 763 he suffered a defeat in the north and it was marked by an eclipse. This also a possible time when Jonah might have come to Assyria.
Ashurnirari	754-745	Also basically a weak king. His greatest claim to fame was his treaty with Mati-ilu in which he

ASSYRIA

Ashurnirari	compared Mati-ilu with a ram. In this comparison he showed vividly what he would do if the treaty was broken.
Pul Tiglath-Pileser 744-727	Brought Assyria back to power. Menahem, king of Israel, out of fear surrendered to him in Arpad. Uzziah formed a large coalition of undefeated cities but the coalition was defeated. While he was busy putting down a revolt in the hills of Urartu, Pekah of Israel and Rezin of Syria invaded Judah in 735. Ahaz appealed to Assyria to come and help him. In 734 Pul came, defeating Israel and then Syria. In 732 he took Damascus and deported the inhabitants to Kir as Amos had prophesied. With Assyria's support Hoshea slew Pekah and became the last king of Israel. Merodach-Baladan submitted to him around 730. The kingdom of the Medes was also defeated and 65,000 people carried off.
Shalmaneser V 726-723	During this reign Hoshea, king of Israel, tried to rebel but relented when threatened by Shalmaneser. Because Hoshea still continued his relationship with So of Egypt, Shalmaneser imprisoned him in 725 and besieged Samaria. The siege lasted three years. In 723 Samaria fell. Shalmaneser is most likely the Assyrian king who took

ASSYRIA

Shalmaneser V		Samaria, despite the claim of Sargon to have taken the city.
Sargon II	722-705	Was the general who claimed the throne when Shalmaneser died. According to one record he was the brother of Shalmaneser. He doubtless was the one responsible for the deportation of Samaria. He claims to have deported 27,290 of the inhabitants of Samaria in his first year. He also claims to have taken the city of Samaria, but this claim is suspect with good reason. Sargon II also invaded Elam, sacked Susa and defeated Merodach-Baladan. During his reign the healing of Hezekiah took place and a delegation from Babylon in 714-713 was sent to Jerusalem to Hezekiah to inquire of the miracle done in the land. Sargon also took Ashdod and Gath in 712-711. Isaiah was told by God to walk naked and barefoot at this time as a sign not to rely on Egypt or Ethiopia. In 710 Babylon rebelled again; and Sargon was again victorious.
Sennacherib	704-681	When Sennacherib became king, Merodach-Baladan rebelled again. Sennacherib became so angry that he took no precautions and foolishly sent his captains and governors ahead of the main army. As a result they promptly

ASSYRIA

Sennacherib

became casualties of war. When the major battle took place he was victorious, but Merodach-Baladan escaped into the swamp. For five days Sennacherib searched in vain for him. To curb his disappointment he describes the joy he felt in plundering Babylon.

In his third campaign in 701 Sennacherib demanded Hezekiah's submission; forty-six cities of Judah had already fallen. In submission Hezekiah paid 300 talents of silver and 30 talents of gold. This was not enough for Sennacherib so he sent his Tartan, Rabsaris and Rabshakeh to deliver terms of surrender. In response God said he would make them hear a rumor and leave. When Sennacherib heard that Tirhakah was coming with a great army he tried to hasten Hezekiah's surrender by another message. The message this time was delivered against God. That night, because they had insulted and blasphemed God, the Angel of the Lord slew 185,000 men of the Assyrian army.

After this, Merodach-Baladan with support from Shuzbu and Kudur-Nahundu rebelled. Sennacherib again was victorious and established his son, Assur nadin shum, as king over Sumer and Akkad. Shuzbu now proved to be the rebel leader. When Assur nadin

ASSYRIA

Sennacherib		shum died, Sennacherib established his youngest son, Esarhaddon, as the king over Sumer and Akkad. In a plot to prevent Esarhaddon from becoming king, Adrammelich and Sharezer killed their father, Sennacherib, while he was worshiping in the house of Nisroch, his god.
Esarhaddon	680-669	Began his reign by putting down the rebellion his brothers had started. He also showed a soft spot in his heart for Babylon in the first year of his reign by turning upside down the decree of Marduk, passed in his father's reign. The significance of this action is understood when it is noted that the number seventy upside down is eleven. The first year of Esarhaddon was also the eleventh year Babylon had lain in ruins. He was the king who colonized Samaria. In battle and in celebrations he showed himself tremendously cruel like his father. He received the title "king of Egypt." Claims to have received tribute from Manasseh. He established Ashurbanipal as the next king of Assyria and Shamash shum ukin as king of Babylon in an effort to prevent future problems.
Ashurbanipal	668-633	Completed the domination over Egypt and Ethiopia that his father

ASSYRIA

Ashurbanipal		had begun. In time his brother Shamash shum ukin rebelled against him. This rebellion was so strong that many of the captains of Ashurbanipal were loyal to Shamash shum ukin above Ashurbanipal. It was probably to Shamash shum ukin that the captains of the king of Assyria took Manasseh to swear allegiance. There Manasseh repented of his evil life and God restored him as king of Jerusalem. In the battle between these two brothers Ashurbanipal was victorious and established Kandalanu as king of Babylon. Ashurbanipal is most noted for two things: for the large library he had and for his tremendous cruelty. Kandalanu may have revolted at his death.
Ashuretililani	632-629	Very little is known about him except that he rebuilt Calah. Assyria began to decline under his leadership.
Sinsharishkun	628-612	In this reign Nabopolassar came to power and drove Assyria out of Babylon in 605. In 614 Nabopolassar joined Cyaxares of Media against Assyria. Assyria fell in 612.
Ashuruballit	612-606	Held out in Haran for two years. In 610 Haran fell and was plundered. Ashuruballit was not there; he had

ASSYRIA

Ashuruballit

gone to Egypt to secure help. Returned to Haran in 609 with the support of a large Egyptian army, yet could not retake the city. In the battle that followed he was captured. The power of Assyria was gone for good.

UNITED KINGDOM

Saul	— 1050-1010 —	Humble at first, later became proud.
David	— 1010- 970 —	Heart was with the Lord.
Solomon	— 970- 930 —	Wise, then foolish, then wise again at end of life.

DIVIDED NATION

Israel

Jeroboam I — 930-909 — He made Israel to sin twenty-one times. From the tribe of Ephraim. Built Shechem, Penuel and Tirzah. He changed: 1. Symbols of religion — golden calves — judgment; 2. Centers of worship — Bethel and Dan; 3. Priesthood — young bullock and seven rams; 4. Religious calendar — changed the month ahead. Son Abijah died as the Prophet Ahijah said. His defeat by Abijam King of Judah made him turn to Syria.

Judah

Reboboam — 930-912 — Showed the foolishness Solomon had worried about. Shemaiah stopped war by a message from God. He followed the Lord about three years. He had eighteen wives and sixty concubines. Shishak defeated him and stripped the temple because of the idolatry and sodomites in the land.

Abijah — 913-910 — Defeated Jeroboam in a battle that killed 500,000 men of Israel. He was

100

Israel	Judah
Nadab — 909-908 — Evil like his father. The curse of Ahijah was fulfilled in Gibbethon when he was killed along with all of Jeroboam's seed by Baasha.	victorious because of his prayer and stand given in 2 Chronicles 13:4-12.
Baasha — 908-886 — Built Ramah because of Asa's reform. Defeated by Ben-Hadad I. Continued in the sins of Jeroboam. Cursed by Jehu the prophet.	**Asa — 910-869 —** Led a tremendous reform. Zerah invaded and was defeated because of Asa's faith and prayer. The Prophet Azariah encouraged him and he led a great revival. He deposed Maacah and burned her idol. Baasha's reaction to this revival was fear. Asa went to Ben-Hadad this time instead of to the Lord. He was rebuked by Hanani; Asa became angry and threw him in stocks. In the last two years of his reign he had a disease in his feet. Instead of turning to the Lord he went to physicians. Yet the Bible says of him that his heart was perfect with the Lord. Ashurnasirpal of Assyria came to power during his reign.
Elah — 886-885 — While drunk he was killed by Zimri, fulfilling Jehu's curse.	
Zimri — 885 — Reigned only seven days. Omri attacked Tirzah and Zimri burned the king's house down upon himself. His death brought more division.	
Tibni — 885-880 — Half the people followed him, he was defeated after five years.	
Omri — 885-874 — Half the people followed him. Purchased the hill of Samaria. Assyrians called Israel land of Omri. He sealed an alliance with Phoenicia by the marriage of his son Jeroboam to Jezebel, daughter of Ethball. He followed in the sins of Jeroboam. Ashurnasirpal came to power	

101

Israel	Judah

in Assyria (883-857), he was very conceited and cruel.

Ahab — 874-853 — As though the sins of Omri were too trivial, Ahab and his wife Jezebel did more evil than all before him. Introduced Baal worship; no longer syncretistic worship but open defiance. Had Jericho rebuilt. Lost his eldest son, Abiram, when he laid its foundation and Segub, his youngest, when he rebuilt the gates; all this fulfilled the curse spoken by Joshua. In judgment for Ahab's wickedness and for the encouragement of the faithful few, God brought Elijah into direct conflict with Ahab. God's judgment was drought for over three years; by the end of the drought Israel was greatly weakened. Elijah then challenged the false prophets of Baal and Asherah. The 450 prophets of Baal showed up at Mt. Carmel. After the prophets of Baal failed to produce fire and God had answered with fire, Elijah had all the prophets of Baal killed. Still, the message of God did not sink in because of Jezebel. Therefore God brought Ben-Hadad of Syria,

Jehoshaphat — 872-848 — Followed the Lord and led reforms, sending teachers throughout Judah. God therefore blessed him with riches and power. His army numbered 1,160,000, not including those stationed in fortified cities. But he did something that became a snare to himself; he made peace with the house of Ahab and married his son Jehoram to Athaliah, the daughter of Ahab and Jezebel. Because of this marriage he was obligated to support Ahab in the battle of Ramath Gilead. When he returned, Jehu the son of Hanani rebuked him severely. He then continued his reforms by placing fair judges and overseers in every fortified city. Later Moab and Ammon invaded the land of Judah. Jehoshaphat turned to the Lord; through Johaziel God gave the answer, "You won't have to fight." When Judah began to sing, Moab and Ammon began to fight Mount Seir and then turned upon each other. Again because of the marriage of his

Israel	Judah
who laid siege to Samaria around 857. Ahab was given terms of surrender and at first accepted them but refused when Ben-Hadad demanded more. Raised an army of 7332 men. By Elijah's promise from God he won the battle; the next year he won again and Ben-Hadad surrendered. Ahab foolishly let Ben-Hadad go, seeing him as a much needed buffer between himself and Assyria. Around 854 Ahab again came directly under God's judgment. Through Jezebel he murdered Naboth for his vineyard. When he heard God's judgment the Bible says he went softly and God postponed the judgment until his son's reign. In 853 Ahab joined Ben-Hadad and nine other cities to fight Shalmaneser III, king of Assyria, at Karkar. The next year Ahab attacked Syria in the battle of Ramath Gilead, defying the words of Micaiah. Jehoshaphat, king of Judah was almost killed but fled; Ahab was shot and died in his chariot. When his chariot returned the dogs licked his blood from the chariot.	son to the house of Ahab he fell into another blunder; he joined Ahaziah the son of Ahab in a ship building project. In judgment God destroyed the ships. Ahaziah was wicked like his father, but not as skilled when it came to military matters. The Moabites rebelled against him and it was left to his son Jehoram after him to bring them back into submission. Again Jehoshaphat joined with the house of Ahab, this time with Jehoram. As the armies were crossing the wilderness of the Dead Sea no fresh water could be found. Jehoram, as a true son of Ahab, blamed Jehovah. Jehoshaphat asked to see a prophet of the Lord; Elisha was brought before them. Elisha rebuked Jehoram but for the sake of Jehoshaphat inquired of the Lord through a minstrel. God promised victory, and true to his word filled the land with water and delivered Moab into their hands.
Ahaziah — 853-852 — Wicked like his father. God destroyed	**Jehoram — 853-841 —** Was wicked because of his connec-

Israel	Judah
the ships that Jehoshaphat had built with him. In his reign Moab rebelled. One day he fell through a lattice window and was seriously injured. He sent to Ekron to inquire of the god Baal-zebub if he would live or die. God had Elijah intercept the messengers and deliver a message of judgment; the judgment was death. Three times Ahaziah sent a company of fifty men to capture Elijah. The first two companies found out that the same God who answered at Carmel could consume them also. The third captain humbled himself and Elijah went with him to deliver his message.	tion to the house of Ahab through his marriage to Athaliah. When his father died, he established the kingdom firmly in his hands by killing his brothers who were more righteous than he was. Under him God brought judgment. Edom revolted as did Libna. Elijah wrote him a letter pronouncing God's judgment upon him for his wickedness. God would bring calamity on his house. The Philistines and Arabs invaded Judah and carried away its riches, his sons and his wives. Only his youngest son Ahaziah remained. Jehoram then died as Elijah had predicted.
Joram (Jehoram) — 852-841 — Since Ahaziah had no son to become king, Joram his brother was next in line. He was the last of the Omri line to be king. Most likely in the first year of this reign Elijah was taken to heaven, and Elisha became his successor. Jehoram was not as evil as his father, as would be expected having seen his brother's end. In his first year he persuaded Jehoshaphat to join him in battle with the king	**Ahaziah — 841 —** As wicked if not more wicked than his father. While Ahaziah was in Jezreel visiting his wounded uncle, Joram, he was mortally wounded in the overthrow led by Jehu. His mother (who was not taken by the Philistines) took over the throne when he died.

Israel	Judah
of Edom against Moab. As the armies crossed the wilderness of the Dead Sea no fresh water could be found. Joram blamed Jehovah. He was rebuked by Elisha, yet given victory because of Jehoshaphat's faith. In desperation the king of Moab sacrificed his eldest son to gain the god Chemosh's favor. Fortunately for him Shalmaneser was keeping Ben-Hadad busy so that for a time he was not under attack from Syria. When Ben-Hadad was finally free from the attacks of 849-848, he made raids into Israel to rebuild his strength. On these raids his right hand man, Naaman, took captive a young Israelite girl. (Then follows the story of Naaman's visit to Elisha to be cured of his leprosy in 846 or 845, probably 845 because of the need for Naaman to lead the battle against Shalmaneser that same year.) In 844 Ben-Hadad again attacked Israel. Elisha warned Israel about Ben-Hadad's every move. Ben-Hadad sent his army to capture Elisha but Elisha captured them instead when God made the whole army blind. In 843 Ben-Hadad again attacked; this time he laid siege to Samaria. When	

Israel	Judah

there was no food left Joram decided to have Elisha killed. Elisha prophesied food and deliverance. Then, in judgment for Joram's intention, Elisha predicted a famine.

Jehu — 841-814 — Anointed King of Israel while in Ramoth-Gilead. In mad haste he returned to Jezreel. Joram, who had been wounded in battle, was anxiously waiting to hear news of how the battle was going. When he saw the chariots coming he sent out some of his men to find out if all was well. When they fell in behind Jehu without returning he told his nephew Ahaziah, king of Judah, and went out personally to see what was going on, suspicious of Jehu's plans. When they met, Joram was killed and Ahaziah was mortally wounded. Aware of what was happening, Jezebel fixed herself up and screamed defiance at Jehu when he entered the gates. To show their submission to Jehu the palace eunuchs threw Jezebel out of the window. Jehu trampled her under his chariot, left her there and went in to eat and celebrate; in the meantime the dogs

Athaliah — 841-835 — the daughter of Ahab and Jezebel. When she learned of her son Ahaziah's death at the hands of Jehu she took over the throne of Judah. To secure it in her hands she killed off all the royal seed. One child of Ahaziah, her own grandson, escaped because Jehosheba his aunt the wife of Jehoiada the high priest rescued him and hid him. They kept him hidden for six years. In Athaliah's seventh year Jehoiada revealed the child and planned his coronation as king. When Athaliah saw what happened in true Jezebel form she screamed out Treason! She was taken away from God's house and killed near the palace.

Joash — 835-796 — His reign is properly divided into two parts. The first part while Jehoiada the priest was alive, the second part after Jehoiada

Israel	Judah
ate Jezebel. To complete his victory and to establish himself as the undisputed king, he challenged the rulers and elders of Samaria to battle. When they would not oppose him he sent another letter requesting the heads of Ahab's seventy sons. The rulers and elders showed their submission by delivering the heads in baskets. Jehu — in Assyrian style — had the heads placed in two piles at the entrance of the city gate as a warning to any who opposed him. He then wiped out the rest of Ahab's children and friends. Completed his rise to power by calling for a mass worship of Baal, demanding that all Baal priests and servants come to his ceremony. He declared that Ahab served Baal a little but Jehu would serve him much. When all were gathered together he murdered them. In place of Baal worship he restored Jeroboam's calf worship. Submitted to Shalmaneser of Assyria and paid him tribute when Shalmaneser attacked Syria in 841, leaving Hazael of Syria to fight without his aid. Because of this lack of support Hazael hated and detested Israel. When Assyria was unable to continue	died. In the first part of his reign he repaired the temple of the Lord. In the second part he turned away from the Lord and became so hardened that when Zachariah, the son of Jehoiada, spoke out against this unfaithfulness, Joash had him stoned to death. In judgment for this action God brought Hazael king of Syria against Judah. Joash was severely wounded, then killed by his own officers.

Israel	Judah
war against Syria because of the revolt of Shalmaneser's son, Syria made war against Israel. The war was so severe that Elisha's prophetic tears were justified.	
Jehoahaz — 812-797 — Like his father Jehu, he worshiped the calf at Bethel. In judgment God allowed Hazael to strike deeply into Israel. So heavy was Hazael's oppression that Jehoahaz's army consisted of 10 chariots and 50 horsemen and 10,000 footmen. In desperation he prayed to the Lord and God gave Israel a deliverer.	**Amaziah — 797-768 —** His reign began well and God granted him a large victory against Edom. In this battle he trusted and followed the words of the Lord, sending home from his army 100,000 Ephraimite soldiers even though he had already paid them. Following the victory, Amaziah bowed down to the gods of Edom! Meanwhile the soldiers he had sent away feeling insulted and angered attacked his land. Full of pride over his victory and full of sin because of his idolatry, Amaziah challenged Jehoash king of Israel to fight him. Jehoash described Amaziah as a thistle that would get trampled; he further told him to be content with his victory over Edom. Amaziah did not listen and as a result was defeated by Jehoash.
Jehoash — 798-782 — Also worshiped the calf at Bethel. Under him the strength of Israel began to revive. Visited Elisha when Elisha was on his deathbed. However, instead of following fully the advice of Elisha to shoot all of the arrows (which would have symbolized total victory over Syria), he only shot three. He therefore won three victories. He also defeated Amaziah of Judah.	
Jeroboam II — 795-754 — Kingdom of Israel reached the peak of its strength under Jeroboam	**Uzziah — 791-739 —** Under the influence of Zechariah he followed the Lord and became

Israel	Judah
II, because of the lack of Assyrian power and the weakness of Syria. Sadly, the same can not be said about the spiritual state of Israel. Hosea described Israel as a cake not turned. Because of this, after his death the nation of Israel collapsed quickly.	very powerful. When he was in his thirty-ninth year of his reign and fifty-five years old he made his son Jotham co-ruler with him. Perhaps the internal strife in Israel following the death of Jeroboam II prompted him to do this. As it turned out it was a wise move. Two years later, in 750, Uzziah desired to burn incense to the Lord in the Holy Place. This rite was given only to the priests. When Uzziah refused to listen to the high priest and eighty other priests who tried to stop him, God turned Uzziah into a leper. His son now needed to function as king. Uzziah still held power but could not function visibly in the role.
Zechariah — 753 — Six-month rule. With him came to an end the blessing which God had given to Jehu; was the last of four generations to descend from Jehu. Assassinated by Shallum.	
Shallum — 752 — Ruled one month. Assassinated by Menahem	
Menahem — 752-742 — During his reign Assyria revived under Pul. Submitted to the Assyrians in Pul's third year. As a result he retained his throne, but had to pay heavy tribute.	**Jotham — 752-732 —** As can be noted by the dating of his reign most of it was spent in co-regencies, the earlier years with his father, the later years with his son. Because of this not much is written about him. He defeated the Ammonites and grew in power because he followed the Lord.
Pekahiah — 741-740 — Continued the pro-Assyrian policy	**Ahaz — 744-728 —** Became a co-ruler while his grandfather Uzziah was still alive. Apparent-

Israel	Judah

Israel

his father had started. Unfortunately for Pekahiah, Pul became occupied elsewhere and Pekah assassinated him.

Pekah — 752-732 — When he took the throne he also backdated his reign to the beginning of Menahem's. Formed an alliance with Rezin and invaded Judah. Ahaz appealed to Pul for help. When Pul came he attacked the land of Israel first and then laid siege to Syria. Because the Assyrians had melted the courage of Israel, Pekah was killed and Hoshea, who submitted to Pul, was his successor.

Hoshea — 732-723 — Last king of Israel. When Pul died he rebelled against Shalmaneser V and courted Egypt's favor through Pharaoh Necho, a petty king of Egypt. Samaria was besieged and taken by the Assyrians.

Judah

ly he was not influenced by his father Jotham or by his grandfather. Ahaz was wicked through and through. A few years after his grandfather died Ahaz took advantage of his father's seemingly weak ability as a ruler and seized the throne from him in 735. In judgment God brought Rezin king of Syria and Pekah king of Israel against him. Instead of taking hold of the promise of God Isaiah delivered, Ahaz turned to Assyria for help. Pul of Assyria responded by defeating some of the cities of Israel and then besieging Damascus. When Damascus fell, Ahaz went to meet with Pul. There he saw an altar and had a copy of it made. This altar he placed in the temple of the Lord and with it changed the religious ceremonies.

Hezekiah — 729-700 — On his reign hangs most of the chronological problem of the Old Testament kings. He was a godly king. In the fourteenth year of his reign he was sick unto death. Because he prayed to the Lord, God added fifteen years to his life. As a sign this would be true God made the

Israel	Judah
	shadow of the sun go backward ten steps. News of this miracle traveled to Babylon, and Mero-dach-Baladan came to inquire about the miracle done in the land. Hezekiah's pride got in the way and instead of glorify-ing God he displayed all his wealth and possessions. Be-cause of this God said all of it would go to Babylon. In the fourteenth year of his second lease on life, in 701, Sennache-rib invaded the land. Because of Sennacherib's blasphemy against God, the Angel of The Lord slew 185,000 Assyrians during the night.
	Manasseh — 699-644 — Very ungodly. Not only did he set his heart to follow false gods, he even murdered the faithful peo-ple who would not follow his example. It is possible that among his victims was the Prophet Isaiah. Because of all this God declared he would execute judgment against Ju-dah. When Shamash shum ukin in Babylon formed a revolt against his brother Ashurbani-pal of Assyria, Manasseh was taken to Babylon. There he re-pented of his sin and turned to the Lord God of his fathers.

Israel	Judah
	God forgave him and had him returned to Jerusalem. His repentance, however, was too late to stop the unfaithfulness he had brought to Judah.
	Amon — 643-642 — Apparently unaffected by his father's change of heart. He followed in all the sins of Manasseh. Assassinated by his own officials. There was apparently a struggle for power that finally resulted in Josiah his son being made king.
	Josiah — 640-609 — Began his reign at the age of eight. This young king would become the most godly king to reign since David. Following the death of Ashurbanipal (633) Josiah, now sixteen years old, began to follow the Lord. Four years later, when Ashuretililani died, (629), Josiah began to purge the land of Judah and Jerusalem. His reform even reached into the fallen land of Israel. In 622 he ordered the temple repaired. During the repair work the Pentateuch was found. Josiah's response was to greatly increase his work of reform. In 609 at the pass of Megiddo Josiah tried to stop the Egyptian

Israel	Judah
	army from reaching Haran to aid the Assyrians. Josiah was killed in the battle.
	Jehoahaz — 609 — The first of Josiah's sons to rule. He reigned only three months. On Pharaoh Necho's return trip to Egypt he removed Jehoahaz as king and appointed Eliakim, another son of Josiah, to reign in his place. Necho changed Eliakim's name to Jehoiakim. Because Jehoiakim was evil Jeremiah said he would not return from Egypt; instead he would die there.
	Jehoiakim — 609-598 — Evil through and through. Hated the Prophet Jeremiah. Took the first scroll Jeremiah had written and cut it up in pieces and then burned it in defiance of Jeremiah and God. In 605 Nebuchadnezzar defeated the Egyptians at Carchemish. Jehoiakim had to surrender to Nebuchadnezzar as he pursued the Egyptians through Palestine. News came to Nebuchadnezzar that his father the king of Babylon had died. In great haste he returned to Babylon to take his throne. In 601 Jehoiakim rebelled after another clash between Baby-

Israel	Judah
	lon and Egypt. Nebuchadnezzar again came against Jehoiakim in 598. Judah as expected was taken. How Jehoiakim died is not known.
	Jehoiachin — 598 — Reigned for only three months and ten days before Jerusalem fell. Nebuchadnezzar deposed him and placed Zedekiah on the throne in his place.
	Zedekiah — 597-586 — The youngest son of Josiah. When Nebuchadnezzar placed him on the throne he changed his name from Mattaniah to Zedekiah. In Zedekiah's fourth year he was summoned to Babylon to swear his loyalty to Nebuchadnezzar. But Zedekiah was not faithful. Instead, he continually flirted with Egypt. Finally, in his ninth year Jerusalem fell. Zedekiah attempted to flee but was captured. Nebuchadnezzar punished him by killing his sons while Zedekiah watched and then blinded him so he would never forget the sight. After this he was taken to Babylon.

APPENDIX

Tables of Kings

KINGS OF ISRAEL — THE NORTHERN KINGDOM

Kings	Reign	Capital	Good Points	Bad Points	Prophet
First Dynasty Jeroboam I	22 years 930-909	Shechem Penuel Tirzah	Abijah his son.	Changed four points of worship.	Ahijah
Nadab	2 years 909-908	Tirzah		Walked in sins of his father.	
Second Dynasty Baasha	22 years 908-886	Tirzah		Tried to build Ramah; walked in the sins of Jeroboam.	Jehu, son of Hanani
Elah	2 years 886-885	Tirzah		Walked in sins of Jeroboam; killed while drunk.	
Third Dynasty Zimri	7 days 885	Tirzah		Committed suicide.	
Tibni	885-880				
Fourth Dynasty Omri	12 years 885-874	Tirzah-6 Samaria	Very capable; made peace with Phoenicia.	Instituted Baal worship; had Ahab marry Jezebel.	
Ahab	22 years 874-853	Samaria	Defeated Ben-Hadad three times; humbled himself at Elijah's rebuke.	Opposed Elijah; killed Naboth; slain in war with Syria.	Elijah, Micaiah, anonymous

115

KINGS OF ISRAEL — THE NORTHERN KINGDOM

Kings	Reign	Capital	Good Points	Bad Points	Prophet
Ahaziah	2 years 853-852	Samaria		Sent to the god of flies; sent three companies to capture Elijah; Moab revolted.	Elijah
Joram	12 years 852-841	Samaria		Walked in the sins of Jeroboam; wanted to kill Elisha in Ben-Hadad's siege.	Elisha
Fifth Dynasty Jehu	28 years 841-813	Samaria		Worshipped golden calves; Hazael invaded.	Elisha
Jeho-ahaz	17 years 812-795	Samaria	Asked help of the Lord.	Left ten chariots under Hazael.	Elisha
Jeho-ash	16 years 798-782	Samaria	Went to Elisha.	Shot only three arrows.	Elisha
Jero-boam II	41 years 795-754	Samaria	Most powerful of Northern kings.	Prosperity bred corruption; followed sins of Jeroboam.	Hosea, Amos
Zach-ariah	6 months 753	Samaria		Evil; walked in sins of Jeroboam.	Hosea
Sixth Dynasty Shallum	1 month 752	Samaria			Hosea

116

KINGS OF ISRAEL — THE NORTHERN KINGDOM

Kings	Reign	Capital	Good Points	Bad Points	Prophet
Seventh Dynasty Mena-hem	10 years 752-742	Samaria		Sins of Jeroboam; paid off Pul.	Hosea
Peka-hiah	2 years 741-740	Samaria		Sins of Jeroboam.	Hosea
Eighth Dynasty Pekah	20 years 752-732	Samaria		Allied himself with Rezin against Judah.	Hosea, Oded
Hoshea	9 years 732-723	Samaria			Hosea

KINGS OF JUDAH — THE SOUTHERN KINGDOM

Kings	Reign	Capital	Good Points	Bad Points	Prophet
Reho-boam	17 years 930-913	Jeru-salem	Listened to advice of Shemiah.	Refused wise counsel; plundered by Shishak, king of Egypt.	Shemiah
Abijam	2 years 913-910	Jeru-salem	In the battle with Jeroboam he re-lied on the Lord and defeated him.	His heart was not perfect with the Lord.	
Asa	41 years 910-869	Jeru-salem	Served the Lord with great zeal; broke down foreign altars; put away sodomites; re-moved his mother from being queen.	Went to Ben-Ha-dad for help against Baasha.	Azariah, Hanani
Jeho-sha-phat	25 years 872-848	Jeru-salem	Very religious; sought the Lord in all things; started a system of public instruction; estab-lished courts of justice.	Made peace with the kings of Israel: Ahab, Ahaziah, Joram.	Elijah, Elisha, Micaiah, Jehu, Jehaziel, Eliezer
Jeho-ram	12 years 853-841	Jeru-salem		Married Athaliah, daughter of Jeze-bel; plundered by Arabians, Philis-tines; Edom re-belled in his reign.	Obadiah, Elijah
Aha-ziah	1 year 841	Jeru-salem		Son of Athaliah; killed by Jehu.	Obadiah
Atha-liah	6 years 841-835	Jeru-salem		Devilish like moth-er; had grandchil-dren killed.	Joel

KINGS OF JUDAH — THE SOUTHERN KINGDOM

Kings	Reign	Capital	Good Points	Bad Points	Prophet
Joash	40 years 835-795	Jeru-salem	Hidden in temple by Jehoiada; cleared the land of Baal worship; repaired the temple; did right all the days of Jehoiada.	Set up idols; had Zachariah son of Jehoiada stoned; Syrians plundered Jerusalem.	Zacha-riah
Ama-ziah	29 years 797-768	Jeru-salem	Did right; sent home 100,000 Ephraimite soldiers; defeated Edom.	But not with a perfect heart; served the gods of Edom; the "thistle king."	Anon-ymous
Uzziah (Aza-riah)	52 years 791-739	Jeru-salem	Set himself to seek God; had a huge army; defeated Philistines, Arabians, Ammonites; greatest extent of kingdom since the split.	Became proud; God smote him with leprosy.	Jonah, Zacha-riah
Jotham	14 years 750-736	Jeru-salem	Ordered his ways before the Lord.	Entered not into the temple of the Lord.	Isaiah
Ahaz	16 years 744-728	Jeru-salem		Reintroduced Baal worship; worshiped Moloch; Judah brought low because of him; sent tribute to Tiglath-Pileser, Pekah and Rezin.	Isaiah, Micah
Heze-kiah	29 years 729-700	Jeru-salem	Began reign with reformation; broke down idols; reopened temple; in sixth year Northern Kingdom fell, but God delivered him from Sennacherib.	Showed the Babylonians all his kingdom.	Isaiah, Micah

119

KINGS OF JUDAH — THE SOUTHERN KINGDOM

Kings	Reign	Capital	Good Points	Bad Points	Prophet
Manas-seh	55 years 699-644	Jeru-salem	He repented and was restored as king.	Most wicked — longest reign; re-built idols Hezeki-ah had destroyed; reestablished Baal and offered his own children; tradition says he had Isaiah sawed in half; tak-en by Assyrians to Babylon.	Nahum
Amon	2 years 643-642	Jeru-salem		Wicked like Manas-seh.	Nahum
Josiah	31 years 640-609	Jeru-salem	Began reign at eight; sought after the God of David; found the book of the Law; reformed Judah.	Attacked Pharaoh Necho of Egypt who was marching against Assyria, died at Megiddo.	Jere-miah, Zeph-aniah, Habak-kuk, Huldah
Jeho-ahaz (*Shal-um*)	3 months 609	Jeru-salem		Deposed by Phar-aoh to Egypt; died there.	Jere-miah, Zeph-aniah, Habak-kuk, Huldah
Jehoia-kim (*Elia-kim*)	11 years 609-598	Jeru-salem		Made king by Phar-aoh; king of Baby-lon bound him in chains; given buri-al of an ass; re-peatedly tried to kill Jeremiah.	Jere-miah, Daniel, Ezekiel, Uriah, Hanania

120

KINGS OF JUDAH — THE SOUTHERN KINGDOM

Kings	Reign	Capital	Good Points	Bad Points	Prophet
Jehoi-achin (*Jeco-niah*)	3 months 598	Jeru-salem		Taken to Babylon where he lived 37 years.	Jere-miah, Daniel, Ezekiel
Zede-kiah (*Matta-niah*)	11 years 597-586	Jeru-salem		Made king by Neb-uchadnezzar, later rebelled; Babylon destroyed Jerusa-lem; his eyes were put out; died in prison.	Jere-miah, Daniel, Ezekiel

121

Destruction of Sennacherib's Army (2 Kings 19:35,36)

122

NOTES

[1] Donald D. Luckenbill, *Ancient Records of Assyria and Babylonia*, Vol. 1, (Chicago: University of Chicago Press, 1968), sec. 438. Subsequent references to this work contain the section numbers, not page numbers.

[2] *Ibid.* 443.

[3] *Ibid.* 445.

[4] *Ibid.* 715.

[5] *Ibid.* 735.

[6] *Ibid.* 740.

[7] *Ibid.* 739.

[8] *Ibid.* 752, 753, 754.

[9] *Ibid.* 816.

[10] Luckenbill, *Ancient Records*, Vol. 2. sec. 55.

[11] *Ibid.* 4.

[12] *Ibid.* 55.

[13] *Ibid.* 63.

[14] *Ibid.* 260.

[15] *Ibid.* 504, 505.

[16] *Ibid.* 650.

[17] *Ibid.* 527.

[18] *Ibid.* 795.

[19] *Ibid.* 385, 386, 387.

[20] Donald J. Wiseman, *Chronicles of the Chaldaean Kings*, (London: Trustees of the British Museum, 1956), pp. 67, 69.

[21] *Ibid.* 69.

[22] *Ibid.* 71.

[23] *Ibid.* 73.

[24] *Ibid.* 73.

[25]Edwin Thiele, *A Chronology of the Hebrew Kings*, (Grand Rapids, Michigan: Zondervan, 1977), p. 57.

[26]*Ibid.* 59.

[27]Edwin Thiele, *The Mysterious Numbers of the Hebrew Kings*, (Grand Rapids, Michigan: Eerdmans, 1965), p. 103.

BIBLIOGRAPHY

Bright, John. *The History of Israel*, Third Edition. Philadelphia: Westminister Press, 1972, 1981.

Finegan, Jack. *Light from the Ancient Past*. Princeton, New Jersey: Princeton University Press, 1959.

Franzmann, Martin H., *Bible History Commentary — Old Testament*. Milwaukee: WELS Board for Parish Education, 1980.

Josephus, Flavius. *Complete Works*. Trans. by William Whiston. Grand Rapids, Michigan: Kregel Publications, 1960.

Keil, Carl F. and Delitzsch, Franz J. *Commentaries on the Old Testament*. Grand Rapids, Michigan: Eerdmans, 1951.

Kraeling, Emil G. H., *Aram and Israel*. Vol. XIII. New York: AMS Press, 1966.

Luckenbill, Donald D. *Ancient Records of Assyria and Babylonia*. Vol. 1 and 2. Chicago: University of Chicago Press, [1968, c 1926].

Olmstead, Albert T. *History of Assyria*. London: C. Scribner's Sons, 1923.

Parrot, André, *Babylon and the Old Testament*. Translated by B. E. Hooke from the French, Studies in Biblical Archaeology No. 8. London: SCM Press, 1958. First English edition 1958.

—————— . *Nineveh and the Old Testament*. Studies in Biblical Archaeology No. 3. London: SCM Press, 1955.

Sayce, Archibald H. *The Hittites*, Second Edition, New York: University Press, 1974.

Thiele, Edwin R. *A Chronology of the Hebrew Kings*. Grand Rapids, Michigan: Zondervan, 1977.

—————— . *The Mysterious Numbers of the Hebrew Kings*. Grand Rapids, Michigan: Eerdmans, 1965.

Unger, Merrill F. *Archaeology and the Old Testament*. Grand Rapids, Michigan: Zondervan, 1954.

_____ . *Commentary on the Old Testament*. Vol. 1. Chicago: Moody Press, 1981.

_____ . *Israel and the Aramaeans of Damascus*. London: James Clarke & Co., 1957.

Wiseman, Donald. J. *Chronicles of the Chaldaean Kings*. London: Trustees of the British Museum, 1956.

Whitcomb, John C., Jr. *Solomon to the Exile*. Grand Rapids, Michigan: Baker Book House, 1971.

White, Ellen G. *Prophets and Kings*. Mountain View, California: Pacific Press, 1917. Ellen G. White Publications, 1943.

Young, Edward. *An Introduction to the Old Testament*. Grand Rapids, Michigan: Eerdmans, 1964.

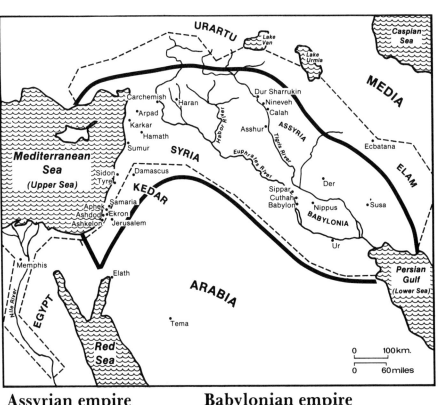

Assyrian empire
11th - 7th century B.C. - - - - - - - - -

Babylonian empire
6th - 5th century B.C. ▬▬▬▬▬▬

The Ancient Near East